A HANDBOOK FOR TEACHERS

····················

Learner Engagement for Academic Success

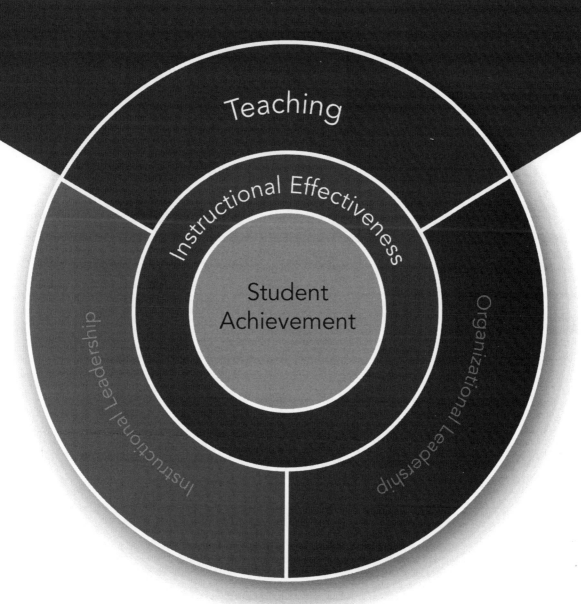

Teaching

Instructional Effectiveness

Student Achievement

Instructional Leadership

Organizational Leadership

**International Center for
Leadership in Education**

RIGOROUS LEARNING FOR ALL STUDENTS

Acknowledgments

The International Center for Leadership in Education
wishes to thank the author of this handbook:

Richard D. Jones, Ph.D.

Copyright © 2012 by International Center for Leadership in Education, Inc.

ISBN-13: 978-1-935300-75-5
ISBN-10: 1-935300-75-X

International Center for Leadership in Education, Inc.
1587 Route 146 • Rexford, New York 12148
(518) 399-2776 • fax (518) 399-7607
www.LeaderEd.com • info@LeaderEd.com

Contents

© International Center for Leadership in Education

 # Overview

The Daggett System for Effective Instruction

The Daggett System for Effective Instruction (DSEI) provides a coherent focus across the entire educational organization on the development and support of instructional effectiveness to improve learner achievement. Whereas traditional teaching frameworks are teacher-focused and consider what teachers should do to deliver instruction, DSEI is learner-focused and considers what the entire educational system should do to facilitate learning. It is a subtle but important difference based on current research and understanding about teaching and learning.

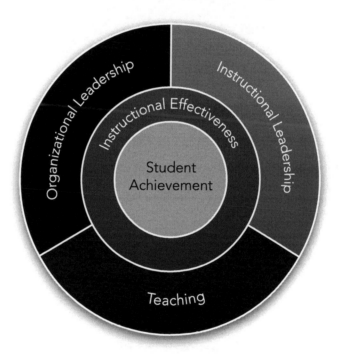

The three parts of DSEI are illustrated here. The following are the critical functions of each part of the system. Think about where you, as a professional educator, fit into this system.

Six Elements of Organizational Leadership

- Create a culture of high expectations.
- Create a shared vision.
- Build leadership capacity.
- Align organizational structures and systems to vision.
- Align teacher/administrator selection, support, and evaluation.
- Support decision making with data systems.

Five Elements of Instructional Leadership

- Use research to establish urgency for higher expectations.
- Align curriculum to standards.
- Integrate literacy and math across all content areas.
- Facilitate data-driven decision making to inform instruction.
- Provide opportunities for focused professional collaboration and growth.

Six Elements of Teaching

- Embrace rigorous and relevant expectations for all learners.
- Build strong relationships with learners.
- Possess depth of content knowledge and make it relevant to learners.
- Facilitate rigorous and relevant instruction based on how learners learn.
- Demonstrate expertise in use of instructional strategies, technology, and best practices.
- Use assessments to guide and differentiate instruction.

When all parts of the system are working together efficiently, teachers receive the support they need, and learners are successfully prepared for college, careers, and citizenship.

DSEI and Learner Engagement for Academic Success

This handbook acknowledges the many ways that learners are distracted and provides practical ideas and strategies for using best practices and technology to keep them engaged in learning. The focus is on ways to improve learner performance on state assessments while learning at high levels of rigor and relevance. This handbook also provides opportunities for professional collaboration to achieve higher rigor and relevance.

Chapter 1: Engaging Today's Learners for Academic Success

This chapter provides useful background about learner abilities and development that helps set the stage for positive steps to achieving learner engagement.

Chapter 2: Building Learner Relationships

Establishing positive relations with learners is an obvious goal, but it is one that cannot be taken for granted. This chapter presents ways to build relationships, describing practical activities to get acquainted, build teams, and reflect.

Chapter 3: Data-Driven Engagement

A key to developing strong learner engagement is to learn how to measure it so it can be developed and improved. This chapter suggests ways to collect and interpret data that measures engagement.

Chapter 4: A School Culture of Engagement

This chapter identifies elements of a positive school culture and discusses its impact on learner engagement. Specific suggestions are given for building a culture conducive to engagement and learning.

Chapter 5: Engagement-Based Learning and Teaching — Preconditions

This chapter identifies preconditions that must be in place before instruction begins: learning relationships, the classroom environment, rewards and grading, guiding principles, learner habits, and fundamental skills. Specific tips and techniques for creating optimal preconditions are presented.

Chapter 6: Engagement-Based Learning and Teaching — Pedagogy

Effective pedagogy makes high engagement happen. This chapter defines and provides tips and techniques for creating pedagogy for rigorous and relevant learning, personalized learning, active learning strategies, and a focus on reading.

Chapter 7: Technology Solutions

Technology can contribute to increasing learner engagement. This chapter explains how technology can be integrated into rigorous and relevant instruction. Practical examples are given.

Chapter 8: Common Problems — Creative Solutions

This chapter provides highly practical and creative solutions to common problems with learner disengagement.

Introduction

Engagement in school is the key to learner achievement. Yet, with the focus on state assessments and the many distractions available to youth today, such as social media and texting, it is no surprise that teachers are facing an ever-increasing number of disengaged learners.

Learner Engagement for Academic Success helps K–12 teachers increase learner engagement by clarifying the essential school preconditions and pedagogy to motivate learners to become active, engaged learners. The handbook is loaded with practical suggestions that will improve learner performance on state assessments and encourage learning at high levels of rigor and relevance. Included are checklists, exercises, and activities to help monitor and increase learner engagement.

Like teaching itself, increasing learner engagement is not an exact science; there is no standard recipe. Still, learner engagement can and should be planned for, measured, and improved. Moreover, learner engagement is not something that just happens because a teacher is assigned a "good" class; rather, it involves a combination of strategies.

Improving learner engagement means helping each learner develop his/her abilities and acquire the cognitive, emotional, and behavioral characteristics of an engaged learner. Engagement encompasses a learner's individual and social needs, and it requires a stimulating environment that is motivating and that stretches the learning process.

Experienced educators know that increasing learner engagement is not easy. Solutions are individual and complex, and they require persistent effort and staff collaboration. The effort, though, is certainly worth it. If we can be successful in engaging learners in rigorous and relevant learning, their futures — and the future of this nation — will be much brighter.

 **Chapter 1**

Engaging Today's Learners for Academic Success

The New Academic Focus: Learner Engagement

With the focus on meeting expectations of state assessments and the many distractions to youth today, ranging from social media to family issues and socioeconomic standing, it is not surprising that many schools are concerned about an increasing number of disengaged learners. This concern has brought learner engagement to the front burner, where it needs to stay if we want all learners to achieve the skills and knowledge that will provide the basis of success and fulfillment throughout their lives.

> What we do doesn't matter nearly as much as how
> kids experience what we do.
>
> — *Alfie Kohn, author*

The purpose of this handbook is to provide strategies and applications to assist K–12 teachers in the intricate task of increasing learner engagement. Once they are engaged, learners have confidence to take action: They are more likely to take rigorous courses and apply higher-order thinking skills, such as analysis and evaluation, to apply knowledge learned in the classroom to real-world, unpredictable situations. They begin to make connections from one content area to the next, and learning becomes both rigorous and relevant. Moreover, learners engaged in the pursuit of academic success not only are learning information in a more productive fashion, but they also are learning how to apply that information — and apply themselves — to the learning process.

Learner engagement refers to the positive behaviors that indicate full participation by the learner in the learning process. When learners are engaged, we can hear, see, or feel their motivation in completing a task, taking pride in their work, or going beyond doing the minimum work required. Engaged learners demonstrate a feeling of belonging by the way they act, the positive things they say about school, and their passionate involvement in class activities.

Experienced educators know that increasing learner engagement is not easy. How many times have teachers (as well as parents and most adults, for that matter) heard learners say, time and time again, "Why do I need to learn this stuff?" Unfortunately, answering the question by saying that they will understand the reason why later in life does little to encourage learner engagement.

Learners need to understand why it is truly important for them to learn something. Teachers should continually work to provide a relevant contextual base for the knowledge and skills they teach to their learners. Education is meaningless and boring when it is reduced to an unending list of content topics for which the learner quickly learns the facts, takes the test, and then forgets it all. Focusing on a narrower list of priority skills and knowledge makes the importance of learning clearer.

Elements That Support Learner Engagement

It is easy to observe the lack of learner engagement when learners are slouched in their chairs and are not listening to the teacher or participating in the classroom discussion. Many teachers who constantly see disengaged learners lament that they could be better teachers and have better learning results if they had the opportunity to work with a "better" group of learners. But classrooms with high levels of learner engagement are not simply a result of "learner quality."

Prior experiences, attitudes, and perceptions affect how engaged learners are in the classroom. But teachers are not limited to poor learning results because learners are not engaged. For teachers to deal with poor learner performance, they must begin to reflect on the elements that contribute to learner engagement. Teachers have direct control and can make changes instantaneously in some areas. For other changes to occur, it will take time to develop new skills for both the learner and the teacher, to plan and seek out new solutions, or to work on making changes at both the classroom and school-wide levels. Following are elements that support and encourage learner engagement.

1. **Cultivate one-on-one relationships.** The one-on-one relationship between learner and teacher is the critical element that can lead to increased learner motivation and higher levels of engagement in academic achievement and school life.

2. **Learn new skills and habits.** Teachers can learn new skills and habits that help them to develop, polish, and enhance their natural inclination to motivate and engage learners.

3. **Incorporate systematic strategies.** Teachers can learn systematic strategies and approaches that facilitate learner engagement. Learners can develop behavioral skills and habits that lead to increased academic achievement and greater involvement in school life.

4. **Take responsibility for learner engagement practices.** It is primarily the teacher's responsibility to engage the learners, as opposed to the teacher's expecting learners to come to class naturally and automatically engaged.

5. **Promote a schoolwide culture of engagement.** The best way to achieve high levels of learner engagement is to develop and maintain a schoolwide initiative that is dedicated to creating a culture of learner engagement, involving learners in school-life activities, and providing a rigorous and relevant education for all learners.

6. **Use professional development to increase learner engagement.** Staff development, combined with staff ownership and recognition, is a critical part of developing and maintaining a culture of effective learner engagement.

Today, all learners need high levels of skills and knowledge to succeed in adult life. Schools must develop a culture of engagement that challenges every learner to achieve rigorous and relevant standards.

New Generations of Learners

The newest generations of youth are the first to be exposed to hyperlinks and global resources that allow them to make multiple connections in seconds. They are accustomed to computers, the Internet, video games, digital music players, texting, and smart phones. As a result of this globalized technological experience, their thinking patterns have changed when it comes to the way that they process information and solve problems. On one level, they have become multitaskers, submerged in a sea of information. Today's youth can surf the Internet, check their e-mail, chat with friends, listen to music, and do their homework at the same time. On another level, they have a highly developed sense of information space; that is, they can intuitively and swiftly navigate back and forth to retrieve the information they need or want. And, they want that information fast! They view textbooks almost as artifacts and have little patience for thumbing through each page of a single-viewpoint source of information.

At some point, educators in today's classrooms will have to admit that learners typically have more information and technology at their disposal than they themselves do. Educators also need to acknowledge that technology will not go away if they ignore it. Still, the "older but wiser" generations of teachers can play an integral role in helping learners realize their futures by providing them with instruction that gives them direction and allows them to hone their new cognitive and technological skills.

In reaching learners who are savvy about and connected to the latest technology, teachers need to ask themselves, "How can we use the Internet, computers, and other technology to enhance instruction and engage learners?"

In high-performing schools, technology is used on a regular basis as a tool, not as a flashy augmentation. In these schools, teachers are fully competent in using technology to engage their learners in the learning process. They access Internet resources, use laser pointers and digital slide presentations, and connect graphic calculators to

TV monitors. For these teachers, technology doesn't sit idle in the classroom; rather, it enhances instruction as a tool, just as a pencil or chalkboard is a tool. Elementary teachers, for example, might use short (under five minutes) video clips to provide learners with visuals to help clarify concepts and bring relevancy to a lesson. Middle- and high-school teachers can turn to the Internet to teach learners how to raise social consciousness of a particular cause and learn about personal responsibility. Again, learners may have more technological ability than their teachers, but they need the content to be fully capable citizens.

Brain Research

The use of magnetic resonance imaging (MRI) is revolutionizing neurological science, especially as it relates to mapping the brain to identify factors that influence people's ability to learn. A scientists can use MRIs to track an individual's brain growth over time and thus gain insight into how the human brain develops from childhood through adolescence into adulthood.

Gray matter is the brain's nerve cells (neurons) and tiny branch-like tributaries, called dendrites. From infancy through early childhood, brain activity and growth occur at the highest levels. Using MRI and other techniques and technology, scientists at the National Institute of Mental Health, the Brain Research Institute at the University of California in Los Angeles, and Harvard University's McLean Hospital have discovered that the brain experiences a second wave of proliferation and the pruning of gray matter, beginning in the prepuberty years and extending into adulthood. Between the ages of 6 and 12, children experience a massive buildup of gray matter, which typically peaks in males at age 12 and in females at age 11. During this time, children develop enormous brain capacity, which allows them to move from being highly skilled dependent learners to novice independent thinkers.

Recent brain research also has revealed that the proliferation of gray matter is followed by a pruning period that lasts for several years. During this stage, white matter, composed of fatty myelin sheaths, thickens and encases the axons of the brain cells, making nerve transmission faster and more efficient.

As scientists delve further into the exploration of the human brain with ever-advancing technologies, they continue to discover just how complex our children really are. On one hand, their brains have a remarkable capacity for learning. On the other, the part of the brain most responsible for allowing rational decision-making is not fully developed, and reactions to situations are dominated by the emotional center of the brain, which is saturated with hormones. These findings further challenge educators to provide stimulating instruction and activities that will foster learning for every learner.

In thinking about learner engagement strategies, remember these three important lessons learned from research on the developing brains of young people.

1. **Use it or lose it.** When youngsters are ages 10–18, the brain ruthlessly destroys its weakest connections, preserving only those that experience has

shown to be useful. The adage here is "use it or lose it" — and this applies at any age. Synaptic pruning continues throughout life but occurs mostly during late childhood and teenage years, so that the synapses that carry the most messages become stronger and the weaker ones eventually disappear.

2. **Youngsters have limited capacity for self-regulation.** In adolescents' brains, the prefrontal cortex — the part that helps people regulate emotions and control impulses — is the last to develop. This is why adolescents often fail to make wise judgments and seem to act without thinking in what we describe as "immaturity." So if the early adolescents' prefrontal cortex has essentially gone missing in action for a time, then teenagers' brains are tuned up for emotions, fighting, running away, and romance, but not so well tuned up for planning and controlling impulses. Young people tend to respond to situations with more emotion as opposed to more executive, thoughtful, and measured responses.

3. **Teenagers tend to be emotionally charged.** Brain research has shown that there is more activity in the emotional parts (limbic system) of the adolescent brain. Adolescents tend to like excitement and are drawn to music, intensity, and horror films. This also means that adolescents learn best when emotion is involved. They remember things about themselves and events relevant to their life situations.

For educators, whose mission is to help each young person under their care to develop to the fullest of his/her potential, the phenomenon of a dynamic and changeable brain, whose health can (to some extent) be cultivated and nurtured, reinforces an intuitive understanding that school can and does make a difference when they:

- create a culture that facilitates positive socialization within a safe, secure, and caring learning environment

- provide opportunities for learners, both in and outside of school, to see the value of participation in physical activity and a healthful lifestyle

- engage and stretch every learner in active, rigorous, and relevant learning that flexes mental muscles and nurtures retention, understanding, and achievement

Gender Differences

There is another critically important aspect of classroom instruction that impacts engagement, according to Susan Kovalik, founder of The Center for Effective Learning. It involves understanding the hardwiring of gender. Girls and boys are different. They see the world differently. They hear differently, and they express their emotions differently. They learn, play, and fight differently. Girls and boys behave differently because their brains are wired differently.

This information is vital, particularly as schools see more and more boys becoming disengaged from the classroom/school. In *Boys Adrift: The Five Factors Driving the*

Growing Epidemic of Unmotivated Boys and Underachieving Young Men, Dr. Leonard Sax contends that a combination of social and biological factors is creating a school environment that is toxic to boys.

All behaviors are on a continuum. Furthermore, each of us is a unique individual, flexible enough to modify our behavior, based on the situation when needed or if motivated to do so. Still, some broad generalizations apply.

Information on gender differences is not new. Over the years, educators have heard about it, but rarely have they applied it with intention in classrooms. Instead, over the past 20 years, schools have focused on creating gender-neutral classrooms/school environments, which in many cases have been detrimental to boys.

In his practice as a family physician and psychologist, Dr. Sax has seen a growing epidemic of underachieving boys. Starting in kindergarten, they are often labeled as inattentive, distracted, and having limited focus. Indeed, they may be put on medication to control such behavior. Dr. Sax's dedication to uncovering what is behind this trend taps into the question of learner disengagement and uncovering the factors that are influencing it.

There is no "right" or "wrong" in this discussion, just the science behind the hardwiring of gender. The past 10 years have proved beyond doubt that classrooms organized around gender-neutral strategies ignore what we have known about our differences. It is once again in the forefront of our thinking as more learners (primarily boys) seem adrift from our classrooms.

The good news is that Dr. Sax recommends alternatives to the traditional classroom approach to help dispel the notion that some learners are not functioning up to par. His books are mainly about boys because their struggle is so obvious; however, he also describes girls' behavior and generally sees it as more conforming at the elementary level because the majority of teachers are female and their classroom strategies reflect their gender. By secondary school, more of the teachers will be male, and more options that have a broader appeal to boys are available.

Hearing and Seeing

Studies have been conducted in an effort to determine whether hearing differences are present at birth or whether they develop over time. Soft music was played in the cribs of some premature babies immediately following birth, and the babies' responses were recorded. These babies were matched in age and weight with other babies without music. Girl babies who received music therapy grew faster, had fewer complications, and were able to leave the hospital 9.5 days earlier than girl babies who had no music. However, boy babies who received music therapy did not leave the hospital any earlier than did boys who did not hear the music.

Another study involved humming to the premature babies. Girl babies who were hummed to left the hospital, on average, 12 days earlier than babies who weren't. Humming made no difference to the premature boy babies.

Hearing is a brain function, and scientists can measure acoustic brain response in newborns and over time. Girl babies have a brain response to a 1,500 Hz tone that is about 80 percent greater than the response of an average baby boy. This is especially important because this range of sound is critical for understanding speech. Other studies have demonstrated that these female/male differences increase as children get older.

The following are some implications for the classroom. Keep in mind that not all boys and girls can be easily categorized by this information, for situations and teacher styles vary. The important thing is to consider the implications that would benefit both boys and girls.

It has been demonstrated that noise levels that distract 11-year-old girls are 10 times softer than noise levels that boys find distracting. Girls won't learn as well in a loud, noisy classroom. If a male teacher speaks in a tone of voice that is normal for him, a girl in the front row may feel that he is yelling. The same may be true when a father is speaking to his daughter. Conversely, males need a loud voice to get their attention. Women often find themselves asking their sons or husbands, "Do you hear me? I'm talking to you!"

Boys will do better if they are in the front of the classroom, where their ability to pay attention increases because they can clearly hear what the teacher is saying. Some boys diagnosed with attention deficit hyperactivity disorder (ADHD) may be distracted when sitting in the back of the room because they can't clearly hear what is asked of them. In classrooms today, especially with youngsters who haven't mastered English yet, some teachers are using headsets to enhance the clarity of speech, and this may assist boys, in general, as well. Seating arrangements in which boys sit in the front and in rows may assist them in listening with intention — and without distraction from peers.

When kindergarten learners are given crayons and a blank sheet of paper to draw anything they want, girls will use multiple colors to draw detailed pictures, usually of people, plants, and animals. In the same class, Matthew is frantically scribbling with a black crayon. "What's that?" asks his teacher. "It's a rocket about to smash into the Earth," he replies. Girls draw nouns; boys draw verbs.

Kindergarten used to be a time of play, building structures with blocks, riding tricycles, and otherwise moving for the better part of the day. Today, seatwork is front and center, where girls see better, and boys are labeled as having an attention deficit for not wanting to finish their worksheets.

Is Risk-Taking Behavior Hardwired?

Many boys enjoy taking risks and are impressed by other boys who do as well. They enjoy the immediate thrill of the risk itself; usually the consequences are not a consideration. Boys are more likely to be seriously injured in a variety of accidents, whether on a bike or skateboard, misusing a gun, or becoming lost in the wilderness. A ranger at a national park reported that 9 out of 10 boys who get lost end up seriously hurt whereas 9 out of 10 girls will be found without serious injury, usually very near the place where they became lost. Girls are willing to take risks but are less likely to seek out risk-taking behavior. Boys overestimate their abilities. Girls underestimate their abilities and will be less likely to engage in an activity in which they have no experience. It may be that when boys choose risk-taking behavior, they find the danger to be exhilarating.

A boy is more likely to take a dangerous risk if other boys are present. If a boy takes his skateboard over a dangerous jump, other boys think that the stunt is awesome. Girls are more likely to ask, "Why would he want to do that?" If a girl does the same thing, other girls would react, "That's crazy! Why would she want to do that?"

Dangerous behavior gives boys a "charge" that is irresistible. Climb the mountain because it is there, ride the bull at the rodeo, become a motocross racer, snowboard down the steepest hill, use alcohol while underage, experiment with drugs — these activities all have a risk to them and produce an emotional high. (Girls participate in these activities as well, but it is not the norm. Some boys do not participate at all because, of course, each of us is unique.)

Emotions, both positive and negative, are processed differently in the brains of boys and girls. Prior to adolescence, there are limited connections between feelings and language in both boys and girls. They may feel mad or sad or disconnected, but they may not be able to describe the feeling or explain it to themselves or others.

Precautions that parents and teachers can utilize when dealing with risk-taking behaviors include three points:

1. Since boys in groups increase their risk-taking without considering possible consequences, try to arrange organized risk-taking opportunities, such as snowboarding or whitewater rafting.
2. Supervised is better than unsupervised. Joining a team — football, soccer, motocross racing — is a supervised risk.
3. Assert your authority. Don't argue. Don't negotiate. Just do what you have to do.

Gender Differences in Classroom Behavior

In the classroom, girls are more likely to do their homework even if the assignment doesn't interest them because they want the teacher to like them. Boys need to find the homework assignment meaningful to them; having the teacher like them is not a necessity. A boy who works well with his teacher may have his status lowered with other boys or may be considered a geek.

When asking for help, girls are responsive to voice, tone, and intention. Boys tend to be more responsive when focusing on the problem only, with little or no eye contact. Small-group learning tends to work for girls because they are more comfortable asking the teacher for help if they need it. If a boy gets stuck, chances are that he won't ask for help and may even become rowdy to get attention. His status in the eyes of the other boys in the classroom is raised if he disrupts the teacher. Competition and time-constrained tasks draw boys' attention. When they have to work as a team to answer a question, they collaborate and work hard so as not to let down the rest of the team.

Girls tend to regard shouting out answers as silly, and they complain that the "right answer" focuses on small details instead of the big picture. Moderate stress improves boys' performance on tests but degrades girls' performance.

What does all this mean? According to Dr. Sax, "Ignoring gender differences does not break down gender stereotypes; ironically, neglecting hardwired gender differences more often results in a reinforcement of gender stereotypes." The solution is not necessarily to have gender-specific classes, although in some situations that has been shown to work very well and is a growing trend in some states. However, knowing about these hardwired differences can inform and direct what we do in the classroom, which will help ensure that learners of both genders are engaged and eager to participate in learning.

Brain-Compatible Teaching

Why do some learners come to school inherently eager to learn but then become disengaged inside the classroom? What makes some young learners who are naturally curious, with active imaginations and eager minds, "tune out" after they pass through the schoolhouse door? Why do other children consistently view school as "fun" and remain excited at the possibilities ahead of them?

The answer lies in the basic but often overlooked reality that learners learn differently, and schools must find effective ways to tap into learners' inherent instinct to want to know and be able to do. Even more significantly, the harsh truth is that learners are expected to learn in ways that are inconsistent with (and frequently the opposite of) the way that learning happens. Instead, they are required to learn in ways that are convenient for the institution and teacher rather than in ways that are brain-compatible, natural, and consistent with their "other" learning — learning that has taken place since birth outside of school, without teaching professionals, textbooks, or worksheets.

What makes a classroom and lesson brain-compatible? Over the past 30 years, research in neuroscience, specifically with the brain, has contributed greatly to our understanding of the phenomena of learning. The following elements provide a brain-compatible guide for classroom instruction:

1. absence of threat
2. meaningful content
3. choices
4. enriched environment

5. movement to enhance learning
6. adequate time
7. immediate feedback
8. collaboration
9. mastery (application)

Interestingly, these brain-compatible elements are the very same elements that attract learners to technology.

1. There is an **absence of threat** at some level where neither peers nor teacher is present.

2. Learners make content **meaningful** using a variety of tools in a combination of ways to suit their individual needs and interests.

3. There are unlimited **choices** in the gathering and presenting of information, and learning becomes interactive and multifaceted.

4. Learners **enrich** their skills as they research, develop, evaluate, and present their information.

5. Learners engage in **physical movement**. Especially because of new interactive technologies, learners can hone skills in snowboarding, golf, tennis, and other sports or play competitive games. It is movement that enhances learning.

   "When we exercise, particularly if the exercise requires complex motor movement, we're also exercising the areas of the brain involved in the full suite of cognitive functions." (John Ratey, *Spark: The Revolutionary New Science of Exercise and the Brain*)

6. Learners are in charge of their own **time** and will work at their own pace as long as their curiosity and interest are sustained.

7. As learners discover/uncover information, there is immediate **feedback**, which allows them to expand their thinking, check other sources, and engage experts where possible.

8. Learners **collaborate/socialize** with those with whom they have something in common, expanding their connections worldwide and paving the way for their future.

9. Learners will stay with a game or project until they have achieved **mastery**.

The good news is that the emerging technology provides a wide range of opportunities for the teacher to engage learners, using their acquired expertise. With the vast array of available technology, it is possible for every subject to have new and dynamic connections, making learning more meaningful and engaging. It is not that learners will not engage; it is that they have chosen what engages them.

 **Chapter 2**

Building Learner Relationships

"Treasure your relationships, not your possessions."

— *Anthony J. D'Angelo*

Positive Relationships — Essential to the Learning Process

The learning advantages are tremendous when learners have positive relationships with their peers and teachers. Whether educators are working with a classroom full of new learners, creating a middle-level team of several classrooms, or starting an advisory session with a small group of learners, it is essential to spend time in activities to build these relationships.

As anyone who has been part of a team knows, the friendships, trust, and dedication among team members do not develop in one session. Everyone on the team needs time to get to know one another and to work together to build a community identity. Following are specific activities to help learners get to know one another, build strong teams, and have fun in reflecting on learning. (Some activities were adapted from other sources. Please see Resources at the end of the chapter.)

Activities for Getting to Know One Another

Alike and Different

Randomly assign learners to pairs. Give learner pairs two minutes to see which pair can list the most items in common (number of siblings, street they live on, favorite sport, favorite meal, and so on). Give a small prize to the winning pair. As an option, you can repeat this with one or two additional pairs. Then have pairs of learners indicate what is different. (Ask that learners not use characteristics of physical appearance.) Finally, ask learners to reflect on the many similarities and differences among all people.

People Bingo

Create a Bingo card with 25 squares. Tell learners to put their name in the center square. Put a question in each of the other squares. (Questions may include "Who has a younger sister?," "Who has traveled outside of the United States?," and "Who was born in another state?" Have learners search for people who meet the criterion of the question and write the name in the square. Give a prize to the first learner whose answers to five questions line up horizontally, vertically, or diagonally.

Ball Toss

Arrange learners in a circle, along with yourself. Explain that you are going to say your name and throw a ball to someone. The person who catches the ball then says, "Thanks, [insert teacher name]. My name is [insert name]" and tosses the ball to someone else. Play continues until everyone has been introduced. Once everyone has been introduced, you can reinforce learner names by having learners call out a name before they toss the ball.

The Story of Your Name

Ask learners to turn to a partner and explain what their name means and where it comes from (if they know). Most learners reveal a surprising amount of interesting information. After partners have worked together, ask each learner to introduce his/her partner to the larger group and explain what his/her name means and where it comes from. You can use given names, surnames, or both for this activity. The greater the ethnic and cultural diversity in the group, the better this exercise tends to work.

Get with the Beat

Assemble learners into a big circle. Say your name, using a motion for each syllable. The entire group then says your name, repeating the motions. The next person says his/her name, with a motion for each syllable. The entire group repeats your name with the motions and then the second person's name with the motions. Continue around the circle.

Balloon Toss

Have each learner anonymously answer these three questions on a small piece of paper.

- What is something *personal* about you that people do not know?
- What is something you are *proud* of?
- What is something *peculiar* about you?

Have learners roll the paper small enough to fit into a balloon and then inflate and tie off balloons with a note inside each one. Have learners toss balloons into the air and keep all balloons aloft. After a minute, tell learners to each grab a balloon, pop it and remove the paper, and then try to find the learner who wrote the answers.

People Puzzle

When forming teams, rather than just assigning groups, make it fun to discover partners. Create (or download) a puzzle with the same number of pieces as there will be learners on a team. Cut the pieces apart and distribute them to the class. Then ask learners to find their partners by matching pieces.

Activities for Building Strong Teams

Birthday Lineup

Have learners line up in order of the month and day of their birth *without talking at all.* You'll find that they will resort to sign language and nudges, that someone might try to start directing with his/her arms, and the like.

Group Knot

Have learners stand in a tight circle, with their hands in the center. Then have learners grab each others' hands at random and hold on. The puzzle is then for the whole group to work together to get themselves untangled without dropping hands. Sometimes the group actually will have formed several smaller circles. You can also divide the class into two or three groups and have them compete to see who gets untangled first.

Encouraging Responses

Give a piece of paper to every learner in the class. Have learners write their name in the center of the page and then pass the sheet to another learner. Everyone has 30 seconds to write one positive statement on each learner's sheet. At each 30-second interval, have learners pass the sheets. At the end, each learner goes home with a sheet filled with encouraging statements.

Blind Obstacle Course

Set up a simple obstacle course that involves items to walk around, step over, and duck under. Working in pairs, one member of each team is blindfolded and must rely on a partner to direct him/her through the course. Learners leading the blindfolded ones must give clear, specific directions. Followers must rely solely on their listening skills to gather information about how to navigate the course.

Team Balloon Bounce

Divide learners into groups of 6 or 8 and have them spread out so that each group has space to work. Holding hands throughout the entire activity, the group's goal is to keep a balloon in the air (for 21 consecutive hits, if possible) using only heads, shoulders, clasped hands, knees, and feet.

Number Lineup

This is a challenge game that can help build cooperation and teamwork. Divide learners into teams (up to 10 members per team). Give each team member a card with a single digit (the numerals 0–9). Give each team a multi-digit number (in which each digit is used only once) and see how quickly the team can correctly line up the people holding the digits.

Puzzle Tag

Divide a group into teams of at least six people. Give each team an easy children's picture puzzle of at least 15 pieces. Mix up each puzzle and place it on the floor or table, a few feet away from the team. The team sends one person to put two pieces of the puzzle together. That person then returns to the team and tags another person to put two more pieces together. Each team member must participate in order. Team members may coach and give directions to the person at the puzzle. The first team to finish its puzzle wins.

Activities for Reflective Fun

Blind Directions

To reinforce the importance of clear directions, set up a situation in which one learner gives directions to another on how to perform a simple everyday task, such as putting on a jacket, wrapping a present, making a peanut butter sandwich, or folding a shirt. One way to do this is to put a screen or divider between the learners so that the director cannot see the follower. Tell the follower to do only and exactly what the director tells him/her to do and to pretend never to have done the task before. Have the class observe and reflect on what was good or bad about the directions and why directions need to be precise.

Quick Review

Five minutes before the end of a class, ask for a quick list of things that learners have learned in that session. Acknowledge each contribution with an encouragement such as "Thank you — that's one!" Giving away small prizes increases the likelihood of getting quick responses from learners.

Alphabet Review

After a unit of instruction or a long reading assignment, divide the class into groups of 3 to 5 learners each. Give each group a sheet of paper with all letters of the alphabet. Have groups list something they have learned in that unit (such as a word, concept, or event) that starts with one of the letters, trying to use as many initial letters as possible. Give a prize to the group that comes up with the most.

Effective Communication

As you build relationships with learners, often it is not what you do but how you do it that has the greatest impact. Communication strategies are important for assigning work and giving feedback to learners in a manner that builds relationships. Following are suggestions on effective communication skills that help build learner relationships.

Timely Talking

The first component of effective communication is deciding to talk at all. Sometimes the decision to engage in a conversation has more impact on building positive relationships than does the actual conversation. For example, by asking a question, giving a compliment, or simply greeting a learner, you can start a conversation that helps to build a positive relationship with the learner.

A teacher must act quickly when a learner exhibits frustration, shows lack of interest, or feels isolated. Also, negative behavior is best corrected with an immediate, direct response. If a teacher fails to speak and acknowledge this inappropriate behavior, then the learner may assume that the behavior is acceptable. Teachers should be constantly aware of the timeliness of their conversations to take advantage of opportunities to build positive relationships, show interest, and assist learners in engaging learning situations.

Tactful Honesty

Poor communication occurs any time a teacher provides inaccurate information, tries to cover up negative events, or shares only part of the "story" with learners. Often this is done in trying to "protect" learners. But the fact is that learners usually get the full story at some point. This lack of full honesty acts as a roadblock to the building of high-quality learning relationships. Learners often indicate that they value teachers who are open and honest with them, and that means sharing both good news and bad.

Still, being honest often can be a significant burden, and full disclosure can be brutal to learners. So while it is important to be honest in talking with learners, it is also important for teachers to use tact. One way to improve tactfulness in conversations is for teachers to be precise in their observations. For example, a teacher observes that a learner is frequently late to class. Rather than commenting that the learner is lazy, irresponsible, or disorganized, it is far more tactful to say to the learner, "You've been late four times this week. That negatively affects the rest of the learners in this class." This comment is still accurate, but less judgmental.

Active Listening

Active listening means focusing on the person with whom you are having a conversation, whether in a group or one-on-one, in order to understand what he/she is saying. It is essential for teachers to practice focusing on learners one on one and engaging in the conversation. Looking directly at a learner and removing other distractions to become more aware of the learner's nonverbal cues are important aspects of active listening. Verbal clues and other observations help to decode a learner's message.

Give each learner time to complete his/her message. Express appreciation for sharing information, and encourage the learner to engage in future conversations. It may be helpful to restate key points to affirm your understanding. Asking additional questions as part of the conversation helps to build this understanding. Avoid making snap judgments; rather, reflect on what has been said and respond appropriately.

Consistent Body Language

Body language is the unspoken communication that occurs in nearly every encounter with another human being. We all have many innate and learned physical characteristics that reveal a great deal about our unspoken thoughts and emotions. Having the ability to read and understand a learner's body language can make a significant difference in the communication strategies that a teacher undertakes. Teachers should learn to read learner body language and recognize the important characteristics that indicate learners' feelings. Teachers also should reflect on their own mannerisms, posture, and gestures that might convey hidden meanings to learners. Following are several tips on how to use one's body effectively in conversations.

- **Eye contact** is critically important. While there are cultural exceptions, good conversation generally requires making eye contact. Eye contact is essential for conveying interest in a conversation.

- **Posture** also conveys a great deal about emotions. Walking around with slumping shoulders or head down conveys a lack of confidence or interest and a generally weak attitude. Learners are not likely to approach teachers who exhibit such negative posture.

- **Head position** is an important indication of confidence. When we are confident, we keep our heads level, both horizontally and vertically. To be more authoritative, keep the head straight and level. Conversely, to be friendly and receptive, tilt the head just a little to one side or the other.

- **Hand gestures and arm movements** also give clues. In general, the more outgoing people are, the more they tend to make big movements with their arms during conversation. The quieter people are, the less they will move their arms away from the body. Try to strike a balance of arm movements to convey friendliness and enthusiasm.

- **Distance** from others is crucial for giving the right signals. Standing too close labels a person as "pushy" or too "in your face." Standing too far away and keeping a distance indicate a lack of interest.

Resources

Gibbs, Jeanne and Ushijima, Teri (2008). *Engaging All by Creating High School Learning Communities*. Windsor, CA: Centersource Systems.

"Group-Building Ideas for 4-H Club and Group Meetings": http://web1.msue.msu.edu/4h/downloads/4-HGroupBuildingIdeas.pdf

Harmin, Merrill, and Toth, Melanie (2006). *Inspiring Active Learning: A Complete Handbook for Today's Teachers, Expanded 2nd Edition*. Alexandria, VA: ASCD.

"Index to Group Activities, Games, Exercises & Initiatives": http://www.wilderdom.com/games/

Scannell, Edward E. and Newstrom, John W. (1994). *Even More Games Trainers Play*. New York, NY: McGraw Hill.

"Teampedia: Tools for Teams": http://www.teampedia.net

 **Chapter 3**

Data-Driven Engagement

Measuring Learner Engagement

A key to increasing learner engagement is finding efficient ways to measure it. When something is measured, summarized, and reported, it becomes important, and people pay attention. Many schools are working diligently to improve learner engagement. Frustration can occur, however, if schools embrace this goal without a systematic approach to measure current learning, set goals, monitor progress, and recognize success.

Some school improvement initiatives such as reading level are carefully constructed, viewed appropriately through the lens of a school's mission, driven by data, and accountable to multiple stakeholders. Other initiatives, such as learner engagement, however, are not so meticulously conceived. Rather than allowing data to drive goal-setting and decision-making, some schools still are guided by good intentions, hunches, and impressions. Often, these schools inadvertently lose sight of learners' needs as they struggle to ensure compliance with state regulations. The quest for learner engagement must be conducted within the context of a comprehensive data system for measuring learning. The same holds true in pursuing the implementation of successful engagement practices that foster learning.

Learning Criteria

Learner engagement, also referred to as student engagement, is one of the four dimensions of the Learning Criteria, a tool created in partnership between the International Center and the Successful Practices Network that supports school improvement processes through data collection and analysis process. The set of criteria was a result of and has become a key part of the International Center's ongoing collaboration to identify and analyze the nation's most successful school practices and policies for achieving a rigorous and relevant curriculum for all learners.

Four Dimensions of the Learning Criteria

The Learning Criteria are arranged in four dimensions that school leaders can use to determine the success of their schools in preparing learners for current assessments and future roles and responsibilities.

LEARNING CRITERIA

1. **Foundation Academic Learning** is achievement in the core subjects of English language arts, math, science, and others identified by the school. Indicators include the percentage of learners meeting proficiency level on state tests and the percentage graduating high school in four years.

2. **Stretch Learning** is the demonstration of rigorous and relevant learning beyond minimum requirements (participation and achievement in higher-level courses, specialized courses, and so on). Indicators include interdisciplinary work and projects, such as a senior exhibition, completing sequences in the arts or career and technical education, and the average number of college credits earned by graduation through dual enrollment. Stretch learning may be the most difficult of the Learning Criteria because it compels schools to define how they are stimulating and stretching each learner, not just the most academically gifted. It challenges a school to find data to validate the claim that "all learners will. . . ." If schools are truly stretching them, learners also will spend most of their time in Quadrants C and D of the Rigor/Relevance Framework.

3. **Learner Engagement** is the extent to which all learners (1) are motivated and committed to learning, (2) have a sense of belonging and accomplishment, and (3) have relationships with adults, peers, and parents that support learning. Indicators include attendance rate and participation rates in extracurricular activities. Learners need to be engaged before they can apply higher-order, creative thinking skills. They learn most effectively when the teacher makes sense and meaning of the curriculum material being taught. This

can happen only if the teacher has created a safe learning environment that encourages learners to meet challenges and apply high-rigor skills to real-world, unpredictable situations inside and outside of school.

4. **Personal Skill Development** consists of (1) measures of personal, social, service, and leadership skills and (2) demonstrations of positive behaviors and attitudes. Indicators include service, learning participation, and teamwork. Think about a son or daughter's new friend. Are you more concerned about the friend's grades, or his/her character qualities? Personal skill development gets to the heart of what makes a citizen, friend, or community member. What are schools doing to promote these qualities? Are they making leadership opportunities available for all learners? Are they creating a curriculum that teaches these skills? Are they making these skills graduation requirements?

The Learning Criteria are designed to provide a robust, comprehensive, and detailed portrait of school performance that clearly maps out a route for school improvement efforts. It delivers data that can fuel accountability reports to the community at large; it underscores the notion that school improvement is a multifaceted enterprise. The Learning Criteria also challenge schools to leverage data as a means of monitoring continuous, long-term growth and improvement efforts.

This model also redefines success in terms that are unique to each school, meets standardized test measures of school success, and reveals the school environment in all of its complexity and depth. It clarifies four important aspects of a well-educated learner and elevates learner engagement as an important measure of school effectiveness. Learner engagement is not the sole purpose of education but an essential part of overall learner achievement and school success. If learners are to retain and apply what they have learned, they have to enjoy the learning process.

Learner Engagement Sample Data Indicators

A school should have data indicators in all four dimensions of the Learning Criteria. Following are some sample data indicators for the Learner Engagement dimension.

For grades K–8, data indicators may include:

- learner surveys
- parent surveys
- learner risk behaviors (asset survey)
- surveys on the degree to which teachers know their learners
- learner participation in classroom and school leadership (Junior Leadership Team and the like)

For grades 9–12, data indicators may include:

- learner surveys
- parent surveys
- learner risk behaviors (asset survey)
- dropout rate
- attendance rate

The specific data indicators used will vary among schools, based upon state requirements and school philosophy, focus, and curriculum. To identify success, all data indicators must be quantifiable in the following four categories:

- **School Performance** — expressed in objective terms
- **Sustained** — trend data to show improvement or maintenance at high levels for 3–5 years
- **Disaggregated** — comparisons in achievement among all subgroups
- **Benchmarked** — compared to similar schools, schools in state, schools in nation, or accepted norms from national/state surveys and reports

The identification of data indicators for the Learning Criteria is the start of a process. It is meant to be dynamic and continuous. Initially, few schools will have all of the data necessary to complete the Learning Criteria fully. It will take time and several steps to move through the process.

Data on learner engagement as part of the Learning Criteria is focused on results or school performance. It does not include measures about education processes and the engagement of learners during regular class instruction. Other instruments can be used for measurement of the level of learner engagement through administrative classroom walkthroughs, peer reviews, or teacher and learner reflection. Process data is important in determining if you are making progress, but you first must commit to focusing on results in learner engagement.

Classroom Walkthroughs

Purpose

Classroom walkthroughs are specific, short observations in classrooms. These may be done by school administrators, instructional coaches, or teacher peers. Classroom walkthroughs are not a traditional supervisory evaluation of the teacher. They are shorter snapshots that focus on a specific instructional practice. They may be conducted by an individual or a team of educators.

Walkthroughs should be introduced after all staff involved fully understand the purpose and expectations. Teachers who will be observed should be contacted beforehand, and the criteria and specific observations that will be examined should be explained. It is important that teachers understand what administrators or coaches will be looking for.

Procedures

All walkthroughs should have a common set of criteria. The purpose of this activity is not to evaluate the teacher but to make classroom observations and talk to learners to obtain specific information about the level of engagement. During a walkthrough, the observer should avoid disturbing the classroom lesson. Once walkthroughs are common practice, teachers and learners will accept them as routine.

Before the walkthrough, observers should introduce themselves briefly to the teacher and obtain any background information that will help them better understand what the learners are engaged in at that particular time. Since the observation is not an evaluation, observers make no judgments nor give any feedback to learners or the teacher. The focus should be on how learners interact with their peers or how engaged learners are in their work. A good rule of thumb is to conduct walkthroughs in classrooms once or twice a month.

After a walkthrough, arrange to have debriefings. These can be handled in two ways. If the intent is to determine the overall learner engagement levels at a school, the debriefing would be for the entire staff, without making references to individual teachers. If the feedback or observation is intended to coach teachers after observing how they conducted their classrooms, then it is important to meet with these teachers individually to discuss the observations made during the walkthrough.

Learner Engagement Characteristics

Many classroom walkthroughs blend measures of learner engagement with measures of instructional practice. Although this is a good way to view effective learning, sometimes we need to pay more attention simply to how well learners are engaged rather than on what kind of instruction is being delivered or how the classroom is set up. In this way, we become focused more on the learner than on the teacher.

The Learner Engagement Walkthrough Checklist that follows examines the degree to which learners are exhibiting engaged behaviors, regardless of what is being taught. This observation is meant to help reach agreement in defining high degrees of learner engagement.

As administrators and instructional supervisors conduct classroom walkthroughs, they can use the checklist to rate the level of learner engagement in each of the categories. The first part is based on direct observation of learners and includes these criteria: positive body language, consistent focus, verbal participation, learner confidence, and fun and excitement. The second part of the checklist requires more than direct observation; it requires talking to learners to determine more about their mental engagement. These criteria include attention to individual needs, clarity of learning, meaningfulness of work, rigorous thinking, and performance orientation.

Several questions for each criterion guide the assessment of the level of learner engagement. Each criterion is rated on a scale from "very low" to "very high." An overall level of learner engagement can be determined by using the compilation of the criteria ratings.

Teachers can use this checklist as a reflective tool to examine themselves and determine the level of engagement in their classrooms. Sometimes it is difficult for teachers to evaluate themselves. However, sharing this checklist with them can help to establish common definitions of highly engaged learners, reflect on practices, and share instructional ideas that contribute to increased levels of learner engagement.

Learner Engagement Characteristics: Part 1

First, the observer must examine the following set of characteristics of engagement. These direct observations include:

- **Positive body language.** Learners exhibit body postures that indicate listening and attention to the teacher and/or to other learners. Eye contact, head position, leaning forward or backward, and positions of arms all indicate a learner's level of interest and attention.

- **Consistent focus.** Learners are focused on the learning activity, with minimum disruptions. Consider these questions regarding learner behavior during the entire observation: Are learners focused on the learning experience? Does their attention waver because of lack of interest, lack of knowledge about how to proceed, frustration, or some outside distraction?

- **Verbal participation.** Learners express thoughtful ideas and answers. They ask questions that are relevant or appropriate to learning. Learner participation is not passive; it involves sharing opinions and reflecting on complex problems.

- **Learner confidence.** Learners exhibit confidence to initiate and complete a task with limited coaching or approval-seeking; they can actively participate in team-based work.

- **Fun and excitement.** Learners exhibit interest and enthusiasm and use positive humor.

Learner Engagement Characteristics: Part 2

The second part of the observation requires conversations with learners to gather details about the degree to which they are engaged in a learning experience. There are five strategies for measuring perception of engagement. For each aspect, questions are provided to encourage conversations with learners.

- **Individual attention.** Learners feel comfortable in seeking help and asking questions.

- **Clarity of learning.** Learners can describe the purpose of the lesson or unit. This task is more comprehensive than describing the activity based on the lesson of the day.

- **Meaningfulness of work.** Learners find the work interesting, challenging, and connected to learning.

- **Rigorous thinking.** Learners work on complex problems, create original solutions, and reflect on the quality of their work.

- **Performance orientation.** Learners understand what quality work is and how it will be assessed. They also can describe the criteria by which their work will be evaluated.

Learner Engagement Walkthrough Checklist

Observations					
	Very High	**High**	**Medium**	**Low**	**Very Low**
Positive Body Language	☐	☐	☐	☐	☐
Learners exhibit body postures that indicate that they are paying attention to the teacher and/or to other learners.					
Consistent Focus	☐	☐	☐	☐	☐
Learners are focused on the learning activity, with minimum disruptions.					
Verbal Participation	☐	☐	☐	☐	☐
Learners express thoughtful ideas, reflective answers, and questions that are relevant or appropriate to learning.					
Learner Confidence	☐	☐	☐	☐	☐
Learners exhibit confidence and can initiate and complete a task with limited coaching; they can work in a group.					
Fun and Excitement	☐	☐	☐	☐	☐
Learners exhibit interest and enthusiasm and use positive humor.					

Perceptions					
	Very High	**High**	**Medium**	**Low**	**Very Low**
Individual Attention	☐	☐	☐	☐	☐
Learners feel comfortable seeking help and asking questions. *Question to Ask:* What do you do in this class if you need extra help?					
Clarity of Learning	☐	☐	☐	☐	☐
Learners can describe the purpose of the lesson or unit. (This is not the same as being able to describe the activity being done during class.) *Questions to Ask:* What are you working on? What are you learning from this work?					
Meaningfulness of Work	☐	☐	☐	☐	☐
Learners find the work interesting, challenging, and connected to learning. *Questions to Ask:* What are you learning? Is this work interesting to you? Do you know why you are learning this?					
Rigorous Thinking	☐	☐	☐	☐	☐
Learners work on complex problems, create original solutions, and reflect on the quality of their work. *Questions to Ask:* How challenging is this work? In what ways do you have the opportunity to be creative?					
Performance Orientation	☐	☐	☐	☐	☐
Learners understand what quality work is and how it will be assessed. They also can describe the criteria by which their work will be evaluated. *Questions to Ask:* How do you know that you have done good work? What are some elements of quality work?					
Overall Level of Learner Engagement	☐	☐	☐	☐	☐

Learner Feedback

Here is a quick and informal way to get feedback from learners on the level of engagement for a specific class period. As you work to increase the level of learner engagement, you will use learner feedback to identify whether you are actually making progress. By involving learners, you also indicate your commitment to make instruction more engaging.

Use the following scale to allow learners to rate the level of engagement. Have all learners give their rating simultaneously and anonymously. (Digital response pads work well for this.) You could also have learners write a rating number on individual cards or whiteboards and then collect them. If you use this technique frequently, you might want to laminate five cards, with the five ratings, for each learner. Learners then would hold up the card with their chosen rating.

Before learners begin to give you feedback, explain the criteria that will be used to rate the level of engagement. A class is highly engaging if learners:

- find the work interesting and challenging
- are inspired to do high-quality work
- understand why and what they are learning
- feel that time passes quickly

Rating Scale

1. Low level of engagement: Class was boring; time moved slowly.
2. Low to moderate level of engagement: Class was OK.
3. Moderate level of engagement overall or high level for a short time: Class was good.
4. High level of engagement for a major portion of the class period: Class was very good.
5. High level of engagement for the entire class period: Wish we had more time.

Four Dimensions of Learner Engagement

Four dimensions of engagement can be used to measure progress in increasing learner engagement.

1. **Verbal participation** refers to learners being eager to share ideas and to ask and answer questions. Are learners confidently sharing ideas and asking and answering questions related to the learning experience?
2. **Body language** refers to how learners exhibit positive body language and make eye contact with others. Does learners' body language show commitment to learn?
3. **Focus** refers to the learners' focus on the learning experience. Are they committed to high-quality work in the learning experience, and do they persevere to completion?
4. **Breadth** refers to how broadly the class as a whole is engaged. Is the entire class engaged? 75%? 50%? Full levels of engagement are not achieved until all learners are engaged.

Following are some suggestions for addressing different engagement scenarios using these four dimensions.

- Low verbal participation
  - Add literacy strategies (such as think-pair-share, idea wave, question cards) to learning experiences.
  - Work on relationships with learners
  - Establish classroom procedures and routines that become habits
- Moderate focus but low breadth (variation throughout the class period)
  - Vary instructional strategies
  - Use active learning strategies
  - Maintain high levels of rigor
- Negative body language
  - Use personalization strategies
  - Work on relationships
  - Integrate instructional strategies that include movement

 Chapter 4

A School Culture of Engagement

An Inviting School Culture

School culture is the observable behaviors and actions of people coupled with the visible aspect of "things" that make up the school community — school building, displays, possessions, appearance, and equipment. What teachers and learners believe, along with their collective behaviors, largely defines the culture. (Administrators also have a lead role in defining school culture.)

The overall culture of a school directly impacts each learner's engagement in learning. An engaging culture seems inviting, exciting, empowering, safe, and comfortable to learners. A school that lacks an engaging culture seems impersonal, cold, unfeeling, overwhelming, and threatening to learners. Such a school can be chaotic, because teacher attention is focused on learner behavior and problems instead of on instruction.

Not all learners will respond to their surroundings in the same manner, but culture does make a difference. People, policies, procedures, community partners, and the physical structures all contribute to defining the school culture and the degree to which it is engaging to learners. The following are components of an engaging culture.

- Interactions between and among learners, teachers, administrators, parents, and so on are respectful, collegial, and warm.

- There is an atmosphere of mutual accountability; people feel a sense of responsibility to one another and to the larger school community.

- Signs of a positive community identity and a sense of belonging permeate the school.

- Learners take leadership roles in representing and "owning" the school, exhibiting energy and enthusiasm about their institution.

- Learners are treated with respect.

- The physical space is clean and safe.

- A strong sense of interconnectedness exists among all stakeholders.

- Regular forums, structures, and interactions acknowledge and celebrate school and individual success.

- The school actively involves and engages family and community members in school life (for example, in learner exhibitions or in a tutoring program).

- Leaders share information that highlights both school successes and challenges, as well as decisions impacting the school, with families and other community members in public forums.

- The school promotes and supports learner activism by helping learners engage in community change.

- The school engages parents and community members in assessing learner work and defining mastery.

- The learning environment is both welcoming and relevant to learners.

- Diversity is valued and encouraged.

Three Key Elements of a Positive School Culture

Many educators accept a school's culture as a given, even though they may become frustrated because the ingrained culture — the "way" of doing things — does not make room for new initiatives and programs that promote a change in structure or learning strategy. However, school culture can be changed to include new ways of encouraging learner engagement practices. To begin this process of change, teachers need to focus on three key elements of a positive, nurturing school culture: practices, conversations, and artifacts (The Education Alliance, Brown University, *Learner-Centered High Schools: Helping Schools Adapt to the Learning Needs of Adolescents*).

1. **Practices** are the individual initiatives that can, over time, begin to influence culture. The success of these practices requires persistence and follow-up.

2. **Conversation** is the most important transformer of school culture. People, and learners in particular, can change what they believe to be true. However, they need an opportunity to express their opinions and to test out new beliefs. Teachers begin to change the culture by cultivating conversations in which ideas can be introduced, challenged, and contemplated. What we talk about in school matters. Teachers can influence beliefs in school by paying attention to the topics of conversation. They can encourage discussion that moves in the direction of the positive culture the school wishes to adopt.

3. **Artifacts** are the tangible evidence of a particular school culture. Examples include academic award banners and displays of learner work. Introduce, move, or replace artifacts to begin to influence the characteristics of the culture.

Addressing Learner Needs

For the culture within a school to change, educators must consider the developmental needs of learners. In summarizing their work in the report *Learner-Centered High Schools,* researchers at Brown University developed a model based on shadowing two dozen learners through their day-to-day class routines and observing eight high schools in New England in which personal engagement is a high priority. The model includes six developmental needs of adolescents:

1. **Voice** is the need to express a personal perspective.
2. **Belonging** is the need to create a unique identity while feeling like part of a group.
3. **Choice** is the need to examine options and select a personal path.
4. **Freedom** is the need to assume increasing accountability for personal actions and their effects.
5. **Imagination** is the need to create a projected view of self.
6. **Success** is the need to demonstrate mastery of adult skills and knowledge.

The six developmental needs of adolescents are aligned with the following six dimensions of school practices:

1. Equity
2. Community
3. Opportunity
4. Responsibility
5. Challenge
6. Expectations

Equity

Equity is the sense that learners are equal parts of the whole. It is driven by learners' need to express their own opinions and feel that they have a sense of worthiness. A negative school culture that demeans certain individuals or creates the impression that learners are powerless, for whatever reason, creates separation and discourages full participation in the school environment. Ways that educators can encourage a sense of equity include the following:

*   Establish forums that provide opportunities for learners to express their opinions.
*   A school newspaper, website, or weblog; special learner events; and focus groups provide opportunities for learners to share concerns, issues, and problems that can be discussed within the wider education community.

- Learner leadership groups, such as the learner council or interclub councils, represent the learner body in a way that creates a sense of equity. Some principals structure learner advisory groups to make sure that all learners are represented when discussing issues and concerns.

- Consistent disciplinary policies and procedures also play a role in equity practices. For example, if athletes or other select groups receive different disciplinary measures for an infraction, learners recognize an attitude of unequal treatment.

- Learners' ideas and concerns should be taken seriously and not dismissed.

- Display artifacts that represent equity, such as schoolwide slogans that show a commitment to equal opportunity for learners and a respect for diversity.

- Ensure that learners with special needs are provided inclusion instruction and assisted to participate in extracurricular activities.

Community

Creating a community in which learners are invited to participate and feel a part of something is essential in establishing a positive school culture. The desire to belong is so strong that unless the school environment creates that sense of belonging, learners will find other — and often troubling — ways to feel that they belong so as to satisfy their needs as human beings.

- Incorporate induction celebrations in which learners are identified, introduced, and welcomed into the school community.

- Longstanding traditions, such as proms, homecoming, and graduation ceremonies, encourage learners to feel that they are a part of a close-knit community.

- Establish welcoming procedures for learners, such as greeting them as they enter the school. A smile and a hello go a long way toward building a sense of community.

- Find ways to include parents as part of the community. Make them feel welcome by providing access to the classroom and by letting them know about school services and opportunities for their children.

- Provide opportunities for meetings that involve the entire school. Small schools, in particular, engage in community-building activities such as morning meetings in which learners and staff share news and other information on a daily basis. In large school environments, look for opportunities to create smaller communities that can meet more frequently.

- To build a sense of community, constantly focus conversations on things that learners have in common rather than on characteristics that differentiate one learner from another. Valuing diversity also is important, however. Learners bring unique experiences and backgrounds to the school culture. In other words, teachers need to show that it is possible to maintain diversity but still share common interests.

- Display school banners and logos throughout schools and identify the unique characteristics of the school.

- Colors can serve as a common identifier. School colors used in a variety of ways — on clothing, bookbags, jackets, or displays throughout the school — reinforce the notion of community.

Opportunity

A school culture should present learners with a number of options to support their need to have choices in the education process.

- Provide learners with multiple pathways to achievement. While it is important to have high expectations and common standards, there also must be varied ways for learners to meet those lofty education goals.

- Not every learner learns at the same speed or through the same kind of activity. The diversity of curriculum moving toward a common set of learning is important in giving learners opportunity. Learners also need opportunities to catch up if they fail to meet academic expectations.

- Support and encourage tutoring options and additional academic programs as ways for learners to meet standards. Extracurricular activities, such as athletics, community service programs, and clubs, also encourage learners to explore their interests and develop their talents.

- Providing leadership opportunities in various activities gives learners the chance to nurture their leadership potential.

- Conversations about opportunity need to focus on the choices that learners make. A primary concern at school is behavior. Learners must recognize that how they behave is a choice. Reminders about appropriate behavior need to begin with learners' recognizing that the choices they make may expand or limit their opportunities.

- Inform learners about the options available to them. Having a large number of athletic teams and extracurricular activities is of little value unless teachers are aware of these options and directly invite learners to participate. It is insufficient merely to distribute a school handbook and assume that learners will choose something. Personal invitation is the best way to encourage participation.

- Make frequent announcements, both verbally and through displays, that emphasize the diversity of expansive opportunities for learners. Events that showcase extracurricular activities or athletic teams help to remind learners of the many different opportunities available to them at school.

Responsibility

Responsibility is the aspect of school culture in which learners can begin to test out adult roles and the need to be accountable for their actions. Responsibility is driven by learners' desire for independence, which can be attained only when they take responsibility for their actions. Schools do a tremendous service when they help learners develop responsibility and move toward increased independence. The following are some ways that teachers can increase learner responsibility.

- Allow learners to negotiate classroom rules and procedures, such as deciding on disciplinary actions.

- Give learners the responsibility for maintaining certain aspects of the school's everyday operations, such as the school's website or other computer and administrative tasks that might be tied to their career interests.

- Conversations about learner responsibilities should encourage learners to assume new responsibilities and/or attempt new initiatives.

- Discussions also need to focus on creating a certain level of trust and giving learners the opportunity to demonstrate responsibility.

- Make learners visible. When they have responsibilities for certain functions in the school, learners should be recognized and praised.

Challenge

When learners are challenged, they feel motivated to tackle difficult work and stretch beyond their previous experience. Children have a natural sense of imagination and creativity. They desire to express their unique abilities and ideas and to achieve some individual recognition. Teachers can feed this desire by creating a challenging and engaging environment.

- The more competitions that are available, the more opportunities there are for learners to rise to the challenge and demonstrate their individual abilities. We know that school athletic competitions challenge learners. Similarly, schools should provide frequent opportunities for learners to participate in academic competitions in a variety of arenas. Teachers also might consider establishing competitions among grades or subgroups.

- Establishing deadlines for assignments is an important aspect of challenging learners. Creating ambitious deadlines for a project or other work sometimes can spur learners to go beyond what they thought they were capable of doing.

- Teachers might pose public challenges that encourage learners to go beyond what they think they are capable of doing. Sometimes, a challenge issued from a "negative" perspective can spur learners to action (for example, "I doubt that all of you can get a perfect score on the quiz").

- Along with public challenges is the important role of private conversations that encourage learners to work harder and to take on more difficult tasks. These private conversations provide learners with support and encouragement for individual success.

- Recognizing learners in visible ways when they achieve success in sports, academics, and other forms of competition is an important artifact in focusing on challenge. Celebrating the success of those individuals shows other learners that they, too, can be recognized if they rise to the challenge.

Expectations

Learners are expected to participate and achieve in school. Their desire for personal success drives them to fulfill such expectations. A school culture should express expectations for learners and help them along the path to success.

- Providing awards is one way to showcase high expectations. These awards need to reflect the objectives and diversity of the school community.

- Recognizing many forms of achievement helps learners envision the different ways in which they can become successful.

- Have incoming learners participate in special meetings that explain what is expected of them in their new environment. Otherwise, learners will just observe and try to figure out what the appropriate expectations might be.

- Plan intake activities, including social activities for learners to get to know one another and programs that introduce mentors to assist them in the new school environment.

- Provide learners and parents with written contracts that explain what their responsibilities are, that clarify behavioral and academic expectations, and that emphasize commitment to learning.

- Schools typically provide a handbook to clarify learner expectations. This written document is useful, but it would be even better if teachers conveyed these expectations to learners in a more interesting or entertaining manner. For example, have learners create skits or visual presentations that demonstrate the expectations and personalize school expectations.

- In conversations about expectations, include stories that provide examples of learners who were successful or who showed great persistence in overcoming initial difficulties. Such messages about achieving success are powerful in conveying to learners the many different ways that they can achieve success in school.

- Teachers can instill expectations in learners simply by making frequent contact with them — calling them by name, asking questions, and talking to them in the hall between classes, after school, and during other activities. Teachers also need to give extra attention to learners who may not be fully participating in the school environment because of family problems or other issues.

 **Chapter 5**

Engagement-Based Learning and Teaching — Preconditions

Introduction

Engagement-based learning and teaching (EBLT) is more than simply telling or encouraging learners to engage themselves in their classwork. EBLT forms the foundation for developing and strengthening learner engagement and the overall learning process. This foundation is built through specific principles, habits, skills, and strategies.

All members of the school community can join forces to develop schoolwide practices that cultivate learner engagement beliefs, values, feelings, motivation, behavioral habits, and skills that are at the crux of high levels of learner engagement.

Regardless of the time it takes to make significant changes that improve learner engagement practices, teachers should become familiar with the two basic elements that, together, provide the roadmap for focusing on and facilitating learner engagement. These elements are *preconditions* and *pedagogy* (which is covered in Chapter 6).

Preconditions are the factors that must be in place even before classroom instruction begins. These factors are:

1. learning relationships
2. creation of the ideal classroom environment
3. rewards and grading
4. guiding principles
5. learner habits
6. fundamental skills

Learning Relationships — Tips and Techniques

Most learners will not do their best in a class when they feel that the teacher does not have an interest in them or care about their future. Learners can sense whether the teacher cares or is simply "going through the motions." Learners show increased effort in classroom activities when the teacher takes an interest in them as individuals, gets to know them by name, and talks to them not only in the classroom but during other activities in the school as well.

Relationship Framework

> The secret in education lies in respecting the learner.
>
> — *Ralph Waldo Emerson*

Learning begins with relationships, and strong positive relationships are critical to the education process. Learners are more likely to make a personal commitment to engage in rigorous learning when they know that teachers, parents, and other learners care about how well they do. They are willing to continue making the investment when they are encouraged, supported, and assisted. Building good relationships complements rigor and relevance. For learners to engage fully in challenging learning, they require increased levels of support from the people around them.

Relationships are not just "good" or "poor"; there are degrees of positive learning relationships. The International Center created the Relationship Framework to help educators understand these degrees of relationships. The Framework consists of seven levels of relationships.

Level 0 is **Isolated**. This is the lack of any positive relationships. The individual feels alone and isolated from social relationships that would enhance learning.

Level 1 is **Known**. A person must know someone before forming a relationship with him/her. Teachers who seek to develop positive relationships with learners first must get to know the learners — their families, likes, dislikes, aspirations, and learning styles.

Level 2 is **Receptive**. A learning relationship often is described in terms of providing the assistance and support that a learner needs. However, a preliminary step is showing that we are interested in and genuinely care about developing a relationship. This comes from frequent contact in multiple settings and from taking an active interest.

Level 3 is **Reactive**. In this case, one person receives guidance or support from another. This relationship yields emotional support and/or cognitive information.

Level 4 is **Proactive**. At this level, people have made a proactive commitment to do more than assist when needed; they take an active interest in supporting the other person.

Level 5 is **Sustained**. Positive support is balanced from family members, peers, and teachers. It is a relationship that will endure over a long period of time. This is the level of relationship that effective parents have with their children.

Level 6 is **Mutually Beneficial**. Although this is the highest level, it rarely is practiced in education. At this point, both parties contribute support to one another for an extended period of time.

The various levels in the Relationship Framework help to identify the changes that need to be made to improve relationships. If a teacher observes that a learner is isolated, the first step is to engage in interventions by getting to the learner and facilitating activities among peers to expand what they know about one another. Just because learners "hang out" together does not mean that they really know much about each other. Sometimes a learner in a group can be just as isolated as the one who sits alone in a school cafeteria.

When relationships are categorized simply as "good" or "bad," teachers are less likely to reflect on practices or make changes. If relationships are "good," there is no need for change. If relationships are "poor," it is easier to blame the learner or to accept things as they are. When a specific framework is used for describing relationships, it has a different effect. Even if relationships are poor, there are at least some positive aspects on which to build.

At the other end of the scale, relationships categorized as generally "good" are usually never as good as they could be. There is the potential for growth and further improvement. All teachers need to continue to work on improving relationships and to strive to reach higher levels.

Relationship-Building Strategies

> The quality of your life is the quality of your relationships.
>
> — *Anthony Robbins, author and motivational speaker*

There are a number of ways to incorporate relationship-building strategies in the classroom. They range from simply "being there" for learners to developing and implementing programs that focus on learner tutors and team-building activities. Teachers can use the following strategies to improve their relationships with learners.

- Show respect
- "Be there" for learners
- Promote one-on-one communication
- Encourage learners to express opinions
- Avoid "put-downs"
- Write encouraging notes
- Encourage learners to praise peers
- Display learners' work
- Identify unique talents and strengths
- Exhibit enthusiasm

- Use positive humor
- Serve as a role model
- Celebrate accomplishments
- Support and encourage social activities
- Participate in team-building activities
- Utilize learners as teachers

Show Respect

Showing learners respect can be as simple as calling learners by their names. When an adult shows interest in what a learner has to say and allows all ideas to be expressed, respect is evident. The tone of voice that a teacher uses in recognizing or responding to learners can greatly influence learners' interpretations of the teacher's respect for them. A learning environment that is characterized by order, a focus on learning, and few disruptions signals respect to the learners. Behavior and activities that encourage diversity and demonstrate the acceptance of different cultures also illustrate respect. Rules about acceptable behavior among learners (such as an intolerance of bullying) provide evidence of respect for learners.

"Be There" for Learners

> Shared joy is a double joy; shared sorrow is half a sorrow.
>
> — *Swedish proverb*

Teachers project an interest in their learners by their participation in and presence at school functions. Learners who notice that teachers are present recognize the value that the teachers place on the learners and their activities. Examples of school events and activities that teachers can observe or participate in to demonstrate their interest include advising extracurricular and cocurricular activities; coaching sports; chaperoning school events; and attending music programs, theatrical productions, and art shows. Teachers also may serve as judges at school competitions.

The presence of teachers in the classrooms before and after school sends a message to learners: Teachers are "there" for them. A teacher who gives learners exact times to meet for extra assistance is telling them that he/she is willing to give extra academic help and is available to do so. Some teachers give learners e-mail addresses and telephone numbers so that learners may contact them if necessary. Participation in after-school, Saturday, and summer academic assistance programs is another example of being present for learners. In some districts, teachers visit learners in their homes, or the district sponsors a door-to-door community outreach to let parents, learners, and community members know that the school values working with youth in the community.

A simple yet highly effective example of "being there" and having contact with learners occurs at the beginning of the school day and during the change of classes. A teacher who greets learners in a hallway establishes a strong contact with learners and sends a subtle message of caring.

Promote One-on-One Communication

One-on-one communication can be powerful in helping learners to express their ideas. Often, learners are afraid to speak in a group out of concern about how others might perceive their ideas. Teenagers do not want to risk being ridiculed. One-on-one communication might mean giving each learner feedback on a recent project during individual learner work time.

Encourage Learners to Express Opinions

Learners have an urge to share their ideas and thoughts, but they often do not have a setting in which they feel comfortable about sharing their opinions. Give learners opportunities to share their opinions and ideas — not only during instruction but at every opportunity for interaction.

Avoid "Put-Downs"

> If Words are the Lyrics, and Laughter the Melody,
> then a Relationship becomes a Symphony.
>
> — *Nicholas Sparks, novelist*

Learners need recognition and encouragement. They seek praise, they want their accomplishments to be noticed, and they want to be validated and recognized for their achievements. "Put-downs," therefore, should not be tolerated. Sarcasm at the expense of another is a form of cruel humor that brings down a learner's self-esteem. Learning is supported by words of encouragement. Showing learners how their work has improved and pointing out specific examples of growth encourage learners to continue to improve.

Write Encouraging Notes

In one school, teachers write each learner a note every month. The note is personal to the learner; it outlines accomplishments and suggests areas that the learner needs to continue to work on in order to improve. The tone and words of the note are encouraging, giving the learner a sense of "Hey, I've done this much, and now I can do more."

Encourage Learners to Praise Peers

"Peer review" is an effective means for learners to praise one another, to develop an understanding of what constitutes quality work, and to interpret exemplars and rubrics. Praise from fellow learners is as valuable as praise from adults in encouraging continued learning and improved performance.

Display Learners' Work

Hanging up or otherwise displaying learners' work for others to see validates their efforts and performance. Displays also send an indirect message to others within the school. The items shown on bulletin boards or displayed in cases serve as examples for others that academic performance is valued.

Identify Unique Talents and Strengths

No road is long with good company.

— *Turkish proverb*

One learner may create well-organized and attention-getting digital slideshows, another may be able to solve complex mathematical equations, and yet another may compose beautiful song lyrics. Recognizing individual talents and academic strengths is not enough: Teachers must also find ways for learners to demonstrate, practice, and "shine" with their unique capabilities. These strategies will further strengthen each learner's sense of potential and nurture continued growth in the recognized area of accomplishment.

Exhibit Enthusiasm

Learners pick up on everything that the adults in the school community say or do — or do not say or do. Enthusiasm breeds enthusiasm. Whether the adults realize it or not, they set the tone and atmosphere of a school; their enthusiasm, humor, ideas, attitude, and behavior are what create the culture of the school.

Use Positive Humor

Humor plays an important role in engaging learners and building relationships. Positive humor brings laughter and creates an "okay" environment. But be careful: Humor that negatively references specific learners, groups of learners, or ethnic groups will reduce the level of positive relationships. Use humor, but be judicious.

Serve as a Role Model

Adults within the school community are the role models for the development of future adults and lifelong learners. There is a famous saying that rings true: "Imitation is the sincerest form of flattery." Learners do imitate the adults they interact with on a daily basis. Adult role models set the norm in school.

Celebrate Accomplishments

The easiest kind of relationship is with ten thousand
people, the hardest is with one.

— *Joan Baez, folksinger and activist*

Celebrations are important in building close relationships among learners and staff members. These occasions can be especially meaningful in developing a sense of community. Some celebrations, such as graduation ceremonies, are held for the school at large. Learners in small learning communities also participate in special events, such as the opening night for an arts academy performance. Celebrations in schools take a variety of forms. There are schoolwide assemblies or special dinners to give public recognition to high-performing learners. Business and community advisory councils also hold celebrations to honor learners for academic achievement or community service.

Support and Encourage Social Activities

At the beginning of the school year, various activities are held by schools to welcome new and returning learners, as well as their parents. Some of the activities include orientation sessions led by learner leaders. These events help familiarize learners with the school's facilities, policies, and procedures.

During this orientation process, the learner handbook is reviewed. Similarly, there might be a dinner meeting for families, at which staff members review policies and opportunities for learners. Other introductory activities may include picnics, pep rallies, welcoming assemblies, skits, and dances. To introduce learners to extracurricular and cocurricular activities, a "club rush" allows representatives to explain the purpose and activities of each organization.

Participate in Team-Building Activities

> You show me a school where learners are working with one another in a caring environment to engage with interesting tasks that they have some say in choosing, and I'll show you a place where you don't need to use punishments or rewards.
>
> — *Alfie Kohn, author*

In academic teaming, teachers are organized, across departments, into teams. Each team shares the same learners and is responsible for the curriculum, instruction, and learner evaluation. The team has common planning time and usually teaches in the same physical location within the school. Teaming adds to the personalization of the learning community. Together, the team members focus on each learner's progress. With teaming, it is easier to focus on the "whole" learner.

Utilize Learners as Teachers

> As 21st century educators, we can no longer decide for our learners, we must decide with them.
>
> — *Ray McNulty, Senior Fellow, International Center for Leadership in Education*

Learning is best remembered when one has the opportunity to teach another. Learners who receive tutoring services, especially from their peers, can succeed at their own level and pace without being publicly compared to more proficient learners. The extra attention and support that learners receive while being tutored generally enhances the support available in the classroom or at home. Research has demonstrated that when learners are provided with appropriate training, they can successfully tutor other learners.

The tutor offers a positive role model for learning and brings enthusiasm in exploring new topics and subject matter. A variety of programs that enable learners to serve as teachers or tutors for other learners exist in schools. These teaching opportunities may occur informally in a classroom setting with a learner who needs academic assistance. There also are cooperative learning activities, in which the group "sinks or swims together" as team members work interdependently.

Many teaching moments occur in this way among learners. In these positive interdependence activities, learners feel that they need one another in order to succeed. Each member of the group is essential in helping to complete the task. When learners perceive that their achievement is correlated with that of other learners, they develop a sense of positive interdependence. Learners recognize that each member functions as a part of the whole and that the success of the entire group depends on the contributions of each member. These team-building activities foster peer tutoring, support, and encouragement.

Some cooperative learning strategies are designed to have learners teach other learners. In an activity called "Line Up," team members divide to learn new information and then teach each other their particular part/topic. In "Jigsaw," academic material is broken down into sections. Each learner is responsible for a part of the information and must learn and teach it to teammates. Cooperative learning strategies create a learning environment in which learners are willing to help one another, give and receive feedback, respect others' ideas, and validate their own ideas. (For more information on these cooperative learning activities, see the work of Elliot Aronson, Spencer Kagan, and Robert Slavin.)

One-on-one instruction has been recognized as superior to group instruction. Learner tutoring programs have many benefits, both to the learners doing the tutoring and to those receiving the assistance. Peer tutoring occurs when the tutor and the person tutored are the same age. Cross-age tutoring has an older learner assist a younger one. Learner tutors may assist with class projects, provide direct instruction, lend support in lab work, help with homework, assist with in-class assignments, discuss ideas with learners, and so forth. In some schools, upper-class mentors remain with learners through 9th and 10th grade and help monitor and celebrate academic success. In other instances, volunteer juniors and seniors are assigned to the freshmen most at risk of failing.

The perceived roles of the tutor include advisor, facilitator, mentor, motivator, friend, peer, team member, communicator, mentor, and role model. The tutors benefit by improving communication and interpersonal skills, reinforcing their knowledge of the subject being tutored, enhancing reflection, increasing self-confidence, and gaining insight into the teaching profession. The learners being tutored receive individual attention from a positive role model, have opportunities to learn more, and obtain assistance in areas of academic deficiency.

Relationships Self-Check

Always	Sometimes	Rarely	
☐	☐	☐	1. I exhibit behaviors that indicate care and concern about learners.
☐	☐	☐	2. I call learners by name.
☐	☐	☐	3. I am familiar with the school community and surrounding neighborhood.
☐	☐	☐	4. I take an interest in learners' education plans and future goals.

Relationships Self-Check (Continued)

Always	Sometimes	Rarely	
☐	☐	☐	5. Learners have opportunities to ask me questions about what they are learning.
☐	☐	☐	6. I talk with parents regularly, including providing positive feedback on learner work.
☐	☐	☐	7. I am willing to provide extra help.
☐	☐	☐	8. I treat learners with respect.
☐	☐	☐	9. I pay attention to all learners, not just to the top learners.
☐	☐	☐	10. I make learners feel that they belong (are accepted and liked) at school.
☐	☐	☐	11. I talk with learners in settings outside of class.
☐	☐	☐	12. Learners feel comfortable enough to ask me questions.
☐	☐	☐	13. I trust learners.
☐	☐	☐	14. My learners work well in groups.
☐	☐	☐	15. My learners treat other learners with respect.
☐	☐	☐	16. I expect learners to do their best at all times.
☐	☐	☐	17. My learners feel supported in doing challenging work.
☐	☐	☐	18. Classroom interactions reflect collaborative working relationships among learners and between me and learners.

Creating the Ideal Classroom Environment — Tips and Techniques

A child is robbed of optimal brain development if
we fail to provide a stimulating environment.

— *Janice Fletcher, education leader*

There is no question that well-designed, well-maintained classroom facilities have a positive impact on learner engagement. Classrooms should be physically comfortable for learners in temperature, space, furniture, and structural organization. Classrooms also need to be mentally stimulating, with attractive displays that include samples of learner work and colorful designs. Good teachers pay attention to the physical learning environment and also to any changes in that environment that become obstacles to learning.

Learning is hard work, and learners are expected to expend significant effort to achieve their learning goals. At the same time, it is the teacher's responsibility to ensure that the school provides an optimal physical setting for learners to engage in their work. Everyone works better in comfortable surroundings. By attending to the physical classroom, teachers can reduce one barrier in the learning process.

You can use the following list to evaluate the organization of the physical learning environment. (Visit www.LeaderEd.com for the white papers "Color in an Optimum Learning Environment" and "The Environment of the Struggling Learner.")

- There are distinct areas for individual, small-group, and large-group activities, or such areas can be easily created.
- The classroom is modified continually to meet the needs of learners and of the work being undertaken.
- The classroom is orderly.
- Provisions are made for learners to work in quiet areas.
- Space is organized to encourage independence for learners by allowing them to find materials on their own and take responsibility for equipment.
- Space is provided to display learner work.

Stimulating the Brain

Learning is a physiological activity that records various stimuli received by the senses. The brain then stores and processes this information. Certain conditions contribute to high levels of brain functioning; others interfere with optimal functioning of the brain. Research has shown that the neurological activity of the brain shuts down when these inhibitors occur. These negative conditions include fear, confusion, inconsistency, and frustration. It is the teacher's role to maximize good learning conditions and remove inhibitors.

- Learners need a learning environment that is free from fear. They should feel safe, both physically and emotionally. A school that has a climate of violence or that tolerates verbal abuse and unruliness cannot produce high levels of learning. On the other hand, positive stimulation improves the functioning of the brain. One of the best methods for stimulating learners is by creating visually attractive and interesting classroom displays. In addition to being varied and colorful, these displays should spark interest and curiosity.
- Use talkativeness as a strength in choosing where to place learners in a classroom. If there is a small-group arrangement, place the most verbally expressive learners in different groups; they will make great leaders. Or consider grouping quiet children together; someone has to emerge! It's also good to give learners some choice in their seating arrangements. For example, invite them to give you the names of six learners with whom they would like to sit. This gives them some control while leaving you the flexibility to make the arrangements work.

- Learners can be territorial about their belongings, so desks with storage areas may pose problems when learners regroup for various activities. As an alternative, have learners keep their supplies in totes that they can take with them wherever they sit.

- The teacher's desk should be located at the back of the classroom. Doing so helps the teacher to promote a learner-centered classroom. By having his/her desk at the back, the teacher has full sight of the entire classroom when using the desk for paperwork.

Following are some common classroom arrangements for various instructional activities.

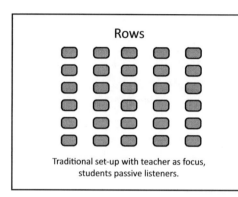

Rows

Traditional set-up with teacher as focus, students passive listeners.

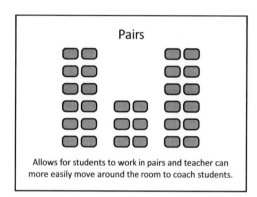

Pairs

Allows for students to work in pairs and teacher can more easily move around the room to coach students.

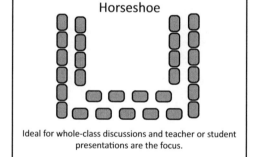

Horseshoe

Ideal for whole-class discussions and teacher or student presentations are the focus.

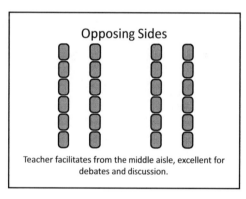

Opposing Sides

Teacher facilitates from the middle aisle, excellent for debates and discussion.

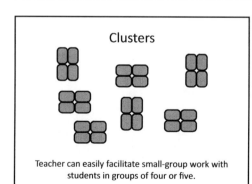

Clusters

Teacher can easily facilitate small-group work with students in groups of four or five.

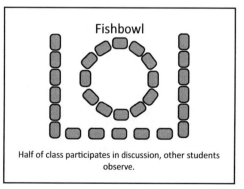

Fishbowl

Half of class participates in discussion, other students observe.

Classroom Self-Check

Always	Sometimes	Rarely	
☐	☐	☐	1. The classroom is colorful and has several mentally stimulating displays.
☐	☐	☐	2. The classroom is clean, and furniture and equipment are well maintained.
☐	☐	☐	3. The classroom seating arrangements facilitate collaboration and discussion.
☐	☐	☐	4. The classroom comfortably accommodates the number of learners.
☐	☐	☐	5. Learners have opportunities to ask me questions about what they are learning.
☐	☐	☐	6. The classroom is free of visual distractions that conflict with learning.
☐	☐	☐	7. Technology is available for information presentation.
☐	☐	☐	8. Internet access is available.
☐	☐	☐	9. The classroom is free of safety hazards.
☐	☐	☐	10. Room temperature is not a distraction.
☐	☐	☐	11. There is evidence of learner work displayed in classroom.
☐	☐	☐	12. Learning goals and objectives are posted.
☐	☐	☐	13. Curriculum standards are posted.
☐	☐	☐	14. Classroom emergency procedures are posted.
☐	☐	☐	15. Communication systems are available to send and receive messages in an emergency.

Rewards and Grading — Tips and Techniques

> Grades are so imprecise that they are almost meaningless.
>
> — *Robert Marzano, education researcher and author*

There is much discussion within education communities and among researchers and practitioners about the role that rewards play in stimulating learner work. Probably every teacher at some point has used a "bribe" of food, recreation, or some other reward to encourage learners to finish a project or to conform to a specific behavior, such as being quiet in a classroom.

There is some concern, and rightly so, that if rewards are used routinely, learners will exhibit the learning behavior only to receive the reward and that when the reward disappears, the behavior will stop. Rewards and incentives do have their place, but they must be incorporated carefully.

A key to the effective use of rewards is whether rewards are offered in advance of a behavior. A bad use of the reward system is when a teacher says to learners, "If you are quiet for the next 30 minutes, you will get a piece of candy." In this scenario, the learner associates the behavior with the reward. It is a better practice to give the reward spontaneously and after the behavior.

Grades are the big incentive system in schools. Learners do the work, but often they do the minimal amount of work possible in order to receive the grade. Some learners even openly avoid doing any work that is not tied to a grade. In this scenario, learners see their learning experiences as meaningless activities, but they have to get the good grade to move on toward the next phase of their lives. Where could learners have gotten this gross misunderstanding of the importance of grades? It is the fruition of how we, as educators, have misguided learners as to what is important. We have tried to spur learner engagement in otherwise boring and meaningless activities by tying it directly to a grade, by giving a reward in hopes that learners would complete their schoolwork.

Moreover, many learners, from prior experiences in school, feel labeled as "C" or "D" learners and see little reason to improve their efforts. Grades are not a motivator to these learners, who are comfortable with completing very little of their work or skipping it altogether. Educators need to reexamine grading policies at both the school-wide and classroom levels to ensure that this reward system creates a situation in which learners are encouraged to work hard.

In general, teachers need to reflect on the appropriate use of rewards in the classroom. The goal should be to build a stronger learner perspective on intrinsic motivation as an incentive for hard work and learning, such as the pride of completing a difficult task or the satisfaction that comes from a job well done. There is no perfect grading system or time to give or withhold rewards. However, schools and teachers constantly need to examine current practices and consider changes that will increase the level of learner engagement without relying solely on grades.

Rewards, Recognition, Incentives

Learner achievement, engagement, participation, and positive behavior are improved through rewards, recognition, and incentives. The recognition of academic success and positive behavior motivates learners to continue to strive toward higher degrees of engagement and academic achievement. Typical incentives used to motivate learners to learn and master new academic content include grading systems, verbal praise and attention, and various tokens and prizes such as stars, coupons, stickers, movie theater passes, discounts at local retail stores, raffle tickets for drawings of special prizes, and so forth.

Kennesaw Mountain High School in Kennesaw, Georgia, for example, has an academic awards program called Vision Quest, which is headed by a learner leadership coordinator. To motivate learners with some additional external symbols of excellence and continuous improvement, the coordinator has created numerous awards, including medallions, medals, certificates, and a wide variety of school-related clothing that can be earned by achieving specific goals. Learners proudly exhibit their accomplishments by wearing shirts and medals that say such things as "Scholar Athlete," "Academic Excellence," and "Academic Success." In essence, Kennesaw Mountain High School has created the same degree of excitement and recognition for academics that many schools have only for athletics.

In *Classroom Instruction That Works*, Marzano and others offer a more subtle approach in referring to the use of the "pause, prompt, and praise" technique to recognize learners who have undertaken a difficult task or question during class time. When the learner looks to the teacher for help with a challenging task, the teacher pauses to give the learner more time to identify, correct, solve, or express the academic difficulty. Following the pause, the teacher provides a prompt or suggestion for the learner to correct an error or to solve the academic difficulty. Finally, after the learner has corrected the error and improved performance, the teacher provides praise for the specific demonstrated achievement.

For incentives to be effective, rewards must be known, and the criteria for receiving them must be clearly understood. Explicit procedures for incentives ensure that rewards are bestowed fairly and objectively. Following are some key points to consider when using a rewards and incentive system in school.

- Rewards should not be based on one learner's performance as compared to another's.

- The rewards are selected because of their appeal to learners. It is important that the rewards correlate to specific learner successes. For example, learners may receive a special award each month for perfect attendance.

- Rewards are based on the attainment of a specific standard of performance.

- Rewards should not be given for merely completing a task.

- The rationale for rewards, incentives, and recognition needs to be established and described to learners. Learners need to understand exactly what they must do to obtain the reward. Learners who do not receive an award have not failed; their performance simply has not met the standard tied to the incentive. This distinction is important for learners to understand, particularly in elementary and middle school. The system should not in any way breed unmotivated or discouraged learners.

- Recognition must be prompt and be provided on an individual learner basis. Receiving accolades weeks after the successful performance is somewhat meaningless to the learner; by that time, the learner has long forgotten the accomplishment. Likewise, general recognition to the entire class for successful performance does not provide individual learners with feedback about their particular attainment of knowledge or demonstrated abilities.

Grading Practices

Grading systems are part of a tradition that can go unexamined and unquestioned for years. The purposes of grades are to communicate progress to the learner and parent, to hold learners accountable for the learning process, and to serve as an incentive for engagement. Following are some key points to consider when using grading systems.

- **Inform learners and parents in advance.** Be sure learners and parents are informed of the grading system in advance of the school year or course. There should be no surprises in what gets graded and its relative importance.

- **Avoid using grades as a reward.** Teachers realize that one of the tools to which most learners respond is the grading system. However, when teachers use grades as bonus points for attendance, good behavior, or doing something extra in the classroom, they actually reduce the importance of grades for academic achievement and fail to communicate the value of learning.

- **Avoid using grades as a punishment.** Likewise, when teachers reduce grades for late papers or take off points for poor behavior, they diminish the value of grades. No research supports the use of low grades or marks as a form of punishment; in fact, instead of prompting greater efforts, using grades as punishment more often causes learners to withdraw from learning.

- **Use separate systems for grading behavior.** Elementary schools have long had the practice of reporting dual grades for subjects — academic achievement and effort. The negative learner behaviors of handing papers in late, not doing homework, arriving late to class, acting out in class, or not having necessary materials can all be translated into a "work habits" grade. In this system, it is appropriate to award points to learners who do additional work. For example, a learner might come in for an after-school tutoring session and erase a tardy designation in the work habits grade.

- **Use incompletes rather than zeros.** Teachers feel obligated to punish learners who fail to do work. Rather than giving zeros to learners whose work assignments are incomplete or not turned in on time, teachers might require those learners to attend after-school tutoring sessions or special Saturday classes until the work is satisfactory. Implementing such a policy may require additional funding and support, but the payoffs likely will be worth it. This approach is more beneficial to learners than simply assigning a zero and letting them "off the hook," and it helps to make grades a more accurate reflection of what learners truly have learned. Not every late assignment should trigger an after-school session. Late or missing routine homework assignments can be handled with daily work habit grades. Learners learn that they have certain responsibilities in school and that their actions have specific consequences.

- **Focus on proficiency.** The grading system should show learners the level of proficiency or competence that is expected of them in various skills and knowledge. Grades should inform learners of their progress toward meeting that level of proficiency.

- **Use systems that reflect the highest level of learner learning.** The goal of instruction is for learners to master certain skills or acquire certain knowledge. The grading system should reflect the gradual development of skills. For example, in an art class, one learner may start with inadequate skills to complete even a basic assignment but then make considerable progress and, by the end of a course, produce outstanding work. Another learner starts with mediocre skills and doesn't improve. If all work in the course is graded equally, the first learner has some low and some high grades while the second learner has all medium grades. Their grade averages might be similar, even though the first learner learned more and achieved at a higher level. A better grading system recognizes the highest level of skill attainment. Remember, objective tests are only inferences of learning.

- **Use performance-based assessments.** Performance-based assessments are quantitative measurements using specific criteria for extended learner work — presentations, report writing, projects, and so on. They compare learner performance to a set standard rather than to the performance of other learners. Learners know exactly what the expectations are. Thus, performance-based assessments are an effective way for teachers to learn whether learners can understand concepts and apply their knowledge. It is not unusual for learners to know all the facts in a particular subject area but fail to understand the connections between the facts or how to use them. Many learners learn by rote with little understanding of *why*, or they draw erroneous conclusions. Well-constructed performance tasks help teachers determine whether their learners really understand the coursework or whether they are merely parroting information that they have memorized. Traditional short-answer tests tell little about how learners think and whether they can use the knowledge or help teachers decide what to teach next.

- **Move toward a proficiency scale and away from percentages.** One of the most nonsensical debates in education circles is what percentage out of 100 should constitute a passing grade. Should 60% be the passing grade? Does 70% mean that learners are learning more? If we drop the passing grade to 55%, are we lowering standards? These questions are meaningless because we are talking about arbitrary numbers that allow us erroneously to assume that there are uniform test questions that measure learning. Current high-stakes assessments do not report results based on percentages, and there is a valid reason for that. Test questions vary in difficulty, and the pattern of questions that learners get right or wrong can be used to varying degrees to approximate learning. A teacher can build an appropriate grading system by translating each quiz, project, assignment, or test into four levels. The overall grading system would then define how much of the learner's work must be at each level to attain that level in each course. To bring this system to some traditional measures in education, schools could designate the grade A or 4.0 for advanced, B or 3.0 for proficient, and C or 2.0 for basic. Schools may or may not want to use a grade of D or 1.0.

Rewards and Grading Self-Check

Always	Sometimes	Rarely	
☐	☐	☐	1. I give frequent verbal feedback about the quality of learner work.
☐	☐	☐	2. I typically make learner praise public and handle learner criticism in private.
☐	☐	☐	3. I routinely use symbols or public displays to recognize high-quality learner work.

Rewards and Grading Self-Check (Continued)

Always	Sometimes	Rarely	
☐	☐	☐	4. Rewards offered in advance as an incentive for hard work are used in moderation.
☐	☐	☐	5. Food, especially high-sugar treats such as candy and desserts, is used as a reward in moderation.
☐	☐	☐	6. I maintain a system for tracking completion of learners' assignments.
☐	☐	☐	7. I maintain a system for information on learner progress in learning.
☐	☐	☐	8. Learners understand my grading system in advance.
☐	☐	☐	9. I communicate frequently with parents about learner progress.
☐	☐	☐	10. I encourage learners to reflect on the quality of their work as part of the grading process.
☐	☐	☐	11. I avoid using grades, such as bonus points, as an incentive for good behavior.
☐	☐	☐	12. I avoid reducing grades as punishment for poor behavior.
☐	☐	☐	13. I use learner contracts for finishing incomplete work or doing additional honors work.
☐	☐	☐	14. Grades reflect the highest level of learner learning and are not simply an average of all work.
☐	☐	☐	15. Grading scales emphasize proficiency rather than the percentage of correct answers.
☐	☐	☐	16. Behavior grades, if used, are separate from academic grading.

Guiding Principles — Tips and Techniques

> Character is like a tree and reputation like a shadow. The shadow is what we think of it; the tree is the real thing.
>
> *— Abraham Lincoln*

Guiding principles are the positive character attributes and appropriate behaviors needed for achieving in school and becoming good citizens as adults. Over the years, however, many schools have moved away from programs that deal with character education to avoid divisive community debates about whether schools should be teaching anything beyond the "3 R's."

The development of a child's character and appropriate behavior is, first and foremost, the responsibility of the family; however, schools, and teachers in particular, can play a strong supporting role. Schools with the highest levels of learner achievement do not sidestep the issue of character education — they embrace it. These schools acknowledge that their success is largely due to their attention to guiding principles. Through guiding principles, such as respect, responsibility, adaptability, honesty, and others, teachers have been able to create the supportive learning environment that is essential if learners are to achieve high standards.

Commonly held guiding principles should be the focus of a school's character-development initiatives. Honesty and responsibility, for example, are both accepted and understood. These principles provide the foundation for learner engagement, as well as for a successful and fulfilled life.

Schools that expect learners to become committed to guiding principles need to assume more responsibility in assisting families in the development of these common core beliefs. The best way to do this is by involving parents in the process, immediately and continually. Educators must not assume that they can determine in isolation what should be taught or modeled. Broad-based involvement by parents, the general public, and educators is essential in identifying and defining the guiding principles to be addressed in school.

The pluralistic nature of U.S. society means that we must approach the teaching of guiding principles differently from nations in which a single religion dominates and thus allows the linking of character education to religion. The United States has many cultures and religions and, therefore, many belief systems. Still, we can teach guiding principles in using common values and virtues without impinging on or promoting specific religious beliefs.

Many schools continue to be paralyzed over issues that relate to attitudes, values, and beliefs. When a district proposes to teach guiding principles, disagreement may arise about whether these principles, and character development in general, are an area in which schools should be involved. However, there is agreement on the importance of having learners possess certain positive characteristics, such as honesty and respect. For this reason, districts should not shy away from community discussions to determine where there is common ground in learner character development. While the International Center is aware of the contentious nature of the subject, character development is too critical to ignore simply to avoid controversy.

Twelve Guiding Principles

> Centering on principles that are universal and timeless provides a foundation and compass to guide every decision and every act.
>
> — *Stephen Covey, author*

The International Center has developed Twelve Guiding Principles of Exceptional Character as a model for schools to draw from as part of their character-development programs. Schools can use this model or devise their own lists of appropriate principles that guide good character. The Twelve Guiding Principles are:

- responsibility
- contemplation
- initiative
- perseverance
- optimism
- courage
- respect
- compassion
- adaptability
- honesty
- trustworthiness
- loyalty

Tips for Teaching Guiding Principles

> Hold yourself responsible for a higher standard than anybody else expects of you.
>
> *— Henry Ward Beecher, 19th-century clergyman, social reformer, and abolitionist*

- Have learners write a "guiding principles" column for the school's newsletter.
- Establish a "guiding principles" resource center in the school library, with books and other materials for learners and parents.
- Have learners discuss a character-based "question of the week" with their families.
- Make a poster that lists learners' names. Every time that a learner does something "honorable" for someone else, write a check mark next to the learner's name. When the learner has 20 check marks, he/she receives a Merit of Honor certificate to take home. In addition, the learner with the most check marks at the end of every month receives a prize.
- Have the class write letters to community service workers to let them know how much learners appreciate them.
- Have learners write a thank-you speech and create an award for a community service worker. Then plan a ceremony in which learners can present their speech and award to their "guest of honor."
- Discuss with learners the value of gratitude during November, when Thanksgiving is celebrated. Each time a learner feels that a classmate has done something nice for him/her, have the learner write it down on a precut heart.

- Reinforce your lesson by asking parents to notice and praise responsible behavior at home. Parents can give hugs or plan special events when children complete score-card activities.

- Have a poster, bumper sticker, billboard, cheer, essay, or poem contest that focuses on one of the guiding principles.

- Introduce one character trait at weekly class meetings. Encourage learners to recognize that trait in others during the week. Talk about what seeing others display that character trait "looks like."

- As a class project, have learners do 100 acts of kindness. It encourages family and community involvement while uniting the classroom community around a common and important goal.

- Have learners create role-playing skits to demonstrate specific traits.

The Ethic of Working Hard

> The quality of a person's life is in direct proportion to their commitment to excellence, regardless of their chosen field of endeavor.
>
> — *Vince Lombardi, football coach*

Working hard in school reflects a passion for learning. Teachers can describe and show their own passion for a particular topic or subject or for learning and education in general. Rather than tell learners why it is important to work hard in school, teachers can help learners ponder on the idea (the guiding principle of contemplation) of working hard. This process fuels self-discovery.

Learners make an enormous number of choices each day. They choose whether to complete a homework assignment, how hard to work on a particular assignment, and how much to study for a test. Each choice can lead to positive behavior and a strengthening of core habits. As with any other aspect of learner engagement behavior, teachers can encourage hard work on homework, projects, and test preparation. They can "catch" and praise individual learners who work hard to do well in school. When learners are working in teams on an assignment, or perhaps when a whole class works together on a project, the team or the class can be praised for its hard work through a special celebration.

Whether the focus is on core habits, guiding principles, or any other cognitive component of learner engagement, learners are bringing together beliefs that stress hard work in acquiring a good education that eventually leads to successful adult roles. This set of beliefs becomes the cognitive foundation upon which teachers can build the emotional and behavioral components of learner engagement.

It is imperative that learners realize why it is important to work hard in school. Too often, they believe that school is merely something to get through and graduate from before they can move on to live their "real" lives. However, working hard academically turns into a pattern of successful lifelong learning and engagement in adult life in endless ways.

Guiding Principles Self-Check

Always	Sometimes	Rarely	
☐	☐	☐	1. I work to decrease detrimental attitudes and behaviors (biases, stereotyping, negative remarks, racial slurs, bullying, gossip, insensitive gender remarks) in my learners.
☐	☐	☐	2. I have learners reflect on character-related issues (using journal writing, essays, class meetings, class discussions, artistic expression, and the like).
☐	☐	☐	3. I give learners opportunities to put guiding principles into action in ways that promote learner autonomy, social responsibility, and caring relationships (for example, through cooperative learning, community service, class meetings, democratic participation, cross-age and peer tutoring, learner governance, and conflict resolution).
☐	☐	☐	4. My instruction integrates guiding principles with academic content.
☐	☐	☐	5. In recognizing my learners, I encourage intrinsic motivation (helping learners recognize the internal "feel good" benefits of positive acts) and discourage reliance on extrinsic incentives (such as material rewards).
☐	☐	☐	6. I encourage parents/guardians to be involved in the school.
☐	☐	☐	7. I use community resources (such as community volunteers, youth groups, business partnerships, and after-school programs and activities).
☐	☐	☐	8. I give learners multiple opportunities (such as surveys, portfolios, projects, and skill demonstrations) to demonstrate their knowledge, understanding, and practice of guiding principles.
☐	☐	☐	9. I understand the school's agreed-upon list of common guiding principles.
☐	☐	☐	10. I prominently display the guiding principles in my classroom.

Learner Habits — Tips and Techniques

> We are what we repeatedly do. Excellence, then, is
> not an act, but a habit.
>
> — *Aristotle*

Classroom habits are the routines and procedures for learners that teachers create. These habits include the way that learners enter a classroom or engage in an activity at the start of every class period. Other habits include the ways that learners open and organize materials that they need for the day, move from large to small groups for various activities, and work on individual problems.

Teachers can improve classroom environments and encourage higher levels of learner engagement if they focus on appropriate procedures and have learners practice until those procedures become habits. When learners fail to follow the procedures, teachers need to remind them of the rules and the ways in which learners can practice them. Good habits help make effective use of instructional time and reduce the disruptions that distract learners from the learning process. It is through practice that these procedures become powerful habits and keep learners engaged in learning.

If we think about the learners we have known, we probably can easily remember those individuals whose habits consistently interfered with their learning. They may have engaged in excessive socializing with friends, playing computer games when they were supposed to be studying, or waiting until the last minute to complete schoolwork. These learners probably did not realize their full academic potential. Similarly, we likely can recall learners whose habits consistently produced a high level of achievement. These learners made a habit of doing their homework, studying for tests, maintaining a positive attitude, actively participating in school life, and doing what was necessary to achieve at a high level.

School, home, and social life compete each day for learners' time, energy, and attention. In an era of the Internet, instant messaging, e-mail, MP3 players, video games, and cell phones, learner distractions can run high. Older learners tend to have part-time jobs and greater access to the society around them, adding to the time that learners may not be thinking about school.

To rein in these distractions, educators can teach learners to recognize, internalize, and apply specific habits that will facilitate academic achievement. Learners need to be surrounded by teachers, parents, and others who encourage engagement by incorporating strategies that:

- provide a basic awareness of habits that lead to high achievement
- help learners learn good habits
- emphasize the importance of good habits
- support the implementation of habits through positive feedback and encouragement

The rapidly developing brains of learners seek to make sense of the world by categorizing experiences. Consequently, learners value rituals and consistent procedures. Kindergarten is all about developing routines and patterns of behavior; these are continued through elementary school but often are neglected as learners move on to secondary school. Teachers can enhance learning if they establish rituals and patterns. For example, try greeting learners as they enter, playing music between activities, and posting thoughtful quotes or intriguing questions. Also, post learner assignments in the same place every day. Identify these in advance and remind learners at the end of each class period. Consistent practicing of routines, beginning in elementary school and extending throughout the high school years, is essential to creating an engaged learning environment.

Successful techniques for transforming beliefs into behaviors include teaching in a way that allows learners to discover ideas about good behavior. One technique, for example, might be the Socratic dialogue approach, in which teachers ask questions that probe for deeper understanding, allowing learners to reconsider their own thinking through self-reflection and relevant knowledge. Teachers also can encourage, prompt, coach, and praise behavior that reflects engagement beliefs and feelings. They can support the emotional component as it is expressed in the form of intrinsic motivation, pride, curiosity, or special interests in a subject or activity. In numerous and different forms, learners can attach positive feelings and associations to learning, studying, completing homework, competing at a high level, and involving themselves in school life.

Bell-Ringer Activities

> Habits are safer than rules; you don't have to watch them. And you don't have to keep them either. They keep you.
>
> —*Frank Crane, Presbyterian minister, speaker, and columnist, late 19th and early 20th centuries*

An excellent way to establish routines for engaging learners early in a class period is to have specific tasks that are expected of learners as soon as they enter the classroom.

- Post on the board a "math question of the day" for learners to answer.
- Provide a paragraph with 10 built-in errors in spelling, grammar, punctuation, or capitalization. Send learners on a hunting expedition. Then review the work with them.
- Have learners in a foreign language class do conjugations, translations, matching, identifying, and so on. Play a song from that culture while they complete the assignment. When the song ends, so does the bell ringer.
- Have learners submit questions on a given topic. The learners whose questions are chosen for use receive rewards.
- Print out short biographies of famous scientists and have learners read a biography on Day 1. On Day 2, have learners write a short summary. On Day 3, have them exchange the summaries and edit each other's work. On Day 4, have them rewrite their summaries and turn in the assignment.

- Choose short current events articles and political cartoons. Have learners explain how each of the choices ties in with what they are studying.
- Use a puzzle, question, paradox, picture, or cartoon on a slide or transparency to focus on the day's topic.
- Give learners a random list of historical events and have them put the events in chronological order.
- Put statements on the board and have learners determine if each is fact or fiction. Keep a running record of how many learners are correct each day.
- Create anagrams or other word puzzles for learners to figure out.
- Have learners write as many words related to a topic as possible.
- Provide a brainstorming activity.

Learner Habits Self-Check

Always	Sometimes	Rarely	
☐	☐	☐	1. I have classroom rules regarding behavior expectations.
☐	☐	☐	2. Classroom rules regarding behavior expectations are posted, taught, reviewed, and reinforced on a regular basis.
☐	☐	☐	3. Classroom routines are consistent and predictable from day to day.
☐	☐	☐	4. I teach, review, and reinforce on a regular basis routines for learners entering, exiting, and moving within the classroom.
☐	☐	☐	5. Classroom rules are stated in positive language.
☐	☐	☐	6. Homework policies are reviewed and reinforced on a regular basis.
☐	☐	☐	7. Learners practice acceptable ways to seek my attention.
☐	☐	☐	8. Learners follow classroom procedures.
☐	☐	☐	9. I use routines for distributing and collecting materials and supplies that result in little loss of instructional time.
☐	☐	☐	10. My noninstructional duties result in minimal loss of instructional time.
☐	☐	☐	11. My responses to learner misbehavior are appropriate.
☐	☐	☐	12. My responses to learner misbehavior are consistent.

Fundamental Skills — Tips and Techniques

> Knowing is not enough; we must apply. Willing is not enough; we must do.
>
> — *Johann Wolfgang von Goethe,*
> *German writer and philosopher*

Fundamental skills are the basic necessities that all learners require to participate in class and complete their work. Learners need basic reading skills, for example, to understand written directions and read materials used in any subject area. Learners also need to acquire the skills to facilitate discussions as a leader and to learn how to listen to the teacher as well as to other learners in group discussions. They need basic skills in technology for doing Internet research or preparing digital slideshow presentations. In addition, learners need to learn basic social skills. To function in the classroom and workforce and to be responsible citizens, they have to learn how to greet others, respect space, ask questions, and resolve conflicts. Teachers should ensure that learners have these skills through conducting preassessment, teaching learners the needed skills, and constantly observing learner engagement levels.

Often, the barrier that keeps learners from becoming more engaged in learning is not attitude or behavior, but rather the lack of one or more basic skills. Many learners are aware that they lack these fundamental skills; however, instead of asking for help, they become embarrassed and withdraw from class. Teachers need to identify learner skills and needs carefully. Sometimes the solution is to teach particular skills to an entire class. At other times, working with individual learners during class or after school is more effective. Following are some skills that learners frequently lack.

Note-Taking

Learners must have the skills to routinely record important information from classroom instruction. Make sure that learners know what is expected for taking notes in your class. Give learners instruction in multiple methods of note-taking, such as the use of graphic organizers, and let them choose the methods with which they are most comfortable.

Many schools use the traditional Cornell note-taking system. The Cornell system is designed to save time and to be highly effective. There is no rewriting or typing of notes; it is a "do it right the first time" system.

Cornell Note-Taking Method

1. **First Step — Preparation**

   Use a large looseleaf notebook. Use only one side of the paper so that you can lay your notes out to see the direction of a lecture. Draw a vertical line 2-1/2 inches from the left side of your paper. This is the recall column. Take your notes to the right of this margin. Later, you can write key words or phrases in the recall column.

2. **Second Step — During the Lecture**

Record notes in paragraph form. Capture general ideas, not illustrative ideas. Skip lines to show end of ideas or thoughts. Using abbreviations will save time. Write legibly.

3. **Third Step — After the Lecture**

Read through your notes and make them more legible if necessary. Now, use the recall column. Use your own words to jot down ideas or key words that give you the idea of the presentation. Cover up the right-hand portion of your notes and recite the general ideas and concepts of the lecture. When you overlap your notes, showing only the recall columns, you have your review.

Memorization

Even if you are on the right track, you'll get run over if you just sit there.

— Will Rogers

Memorization still has a place in school. Learners should understand that some information is most efficiently accessed through direct recall rather than through looking it up in a reference source.

There are many techniques for remembering information. Some learners learn information by using mnemonic devices to connect key information, such as making the first letter in a series of words into a new word that is easy to remember. Learners also can use visual images to memorize information.

There are three main components in memorization:

- using multiple senses
- making an association interesting or familiar
- associating items to something already known

Multiple-sensory instruction and interesting relevant instruction will aid in memory. In addition, the use of memorization techniques, or mnemonics, will create associations that will enable learners to recall critical and important information.

Don't confuse memorizing with comprehending. Teachers might have learners memorize dates for a history class or formulas for a math class, but learners also need to understand why a date or a formula is significant to the key ideas of the material being taught. Before spending vast amounts of time having learners memorize details, teachers should ask themselves if it would be better to step back and focus on overall comprehension of the big picture.

Creative or silly mnemonics often work best because they are easy to remember. Exaggerate size and choose unlikely functions for the image. Here are some suggestions to help learners create their own mnemonics.

- Create your own mnemonics, based on your own vivid pictures.
- Use positive, pleasant images. The brain often blocks out unpleasant ones.
- Closing your eyes while trying to visualize an image or story will make it more vivid.
- Be humorous! Funny or peculiar things are easier to remember than normal ones.
- Symbols (red traffic lights, pointing fingers) can be used in mnemonics.
- Tying a string around your finger really does work.
- Colorful images are easier to remember than drab ones.
- Use all the senses to code information or to dress up an image.
- Remember that your mnemonic can contain sounds, smells, tastes, touch, movements, and feelings, as well as pictures.
- Bringing three dimensions and movement to an image makes it more vivid. Movement can be used either to maintain the flow of association or to help learners remember actions.
- Remember to use a unique location for each list to separate similar mnemonics. By setting a mnemonic story in one location and clearly using that location as a background, you can separate it from a different mnemonic set in a different place.
- When learning new vocabulary words, use a mnemonic to remember the terms.

Active Listening

As discussed in previous sections, active listening means "listening for meaning." The listener checks with the speaker to see that a statement has been correctly heard and understood. The goal of active listening is to improve mutual understanding. When interacting, people often are not listening attentively to one another. They may be distracted or be thinking about what they are going to say next. (The latter case is particularly true in conflict situations or disagreements.)

Active listening is a structured way of listening and responding. It focuses attention on the speaker. Suspending judgment is important in order to attend fully to the speaker. It also is important to observe the other person's behavior and body language. After listening to the speaker, the listener may then paraphrase the speaker's words. The listener does not have to agree with the speaker; what is important is that he or she understands what has been said. In emotionally charged communications, the listener may listen for feelings. Thus, rather than merely repeating what the speaker has said, the active listener might describe the underlying emotion (such as

"You seem to be angry" or "You seem to feel frustrated. Is that because . . . ?"). An active listener needs to focus full attention on the person who is speaking.

Ways in which learners can show that they are actively listening include:

- asking good questions
- listening in a nonjudgmental way
- paraphrasing
- empathizing with the speaker

Cognitive Structures

In her book *Getting to Got It!: Helping Struggling Learners Learn How to Learn*, Betty Garner describes the importance of "cognitive structures" as the missing link and the reason that many learners are not able to handle higher-level thinking and challenging work in school. Cognitive structures might be considered habits of thinking, and they certainly are fundamental skills that enhance learners' ability to engage fully in learning. Just as poor reading skills are an obstacle to learning, lack of cognitive structures can be obstacles to learning. Still, even learners who lack these skills in middle and high school can acquire them.

Teachers need to look for learners who are struggling to acquire new information or solve problems and then teach them in a way that develops these fundamental skills that encompass critical habits of thinking.

Garner describes eight cognitive structures that learners should possess.

1. **Recognition** is the ability to observe consistent patterns in identifying something that has been seen before, such as when an infant recognizes his/her mother. Spend time having learners carefully observe words, images, events, text, and activities to define patterns that are similar to previous observations. Learners cannot compare and contrast if they don't first develop skills to fully recognize the world around them.

2. **Memorization** is the ability to store information so that it can be retrieved. Teachers can help learners memorize by having them reflect on connecting new information with prior knowledge and on arranging new information in a way that creates an easily recalled pattern.

3. **Conservation of constancy** is the ability to understand why some things change and others remain constant. This ability is key to understanding how words change when used in different tenses or with prefixes or suffixes. For example, 1/2 is the same as 4/8, and *regular* is different from *irregular*. Teachers help learners establish conservation of constancy by frequently having them compare items that are similar but seem different.

4. **Classification** is the ability to compare and order information to establish meaning on the basis of comparing a part or parts to the whole. To classify, learners need to create and/or apply a set of criteria to the objects to classify.

Often, it is better for learners to create their own criteria, for they remember them better. Instead of frequently giving learners a blank graphic organizer template, have them create their own to develop their classification skills.

5. **Spatial orientation** is the ability to identify relationships between objects and places. This can include physical space (real objects and places), representational space (mathematics, game strategy, and art) and abstract space (mental models). Teachers can help learners strengthen their spatial orientation by frequently reminding them of relationships between objects and geographic directions.

6. **Temporal orientation** is the ability to process events in regard to when they occur. When learners can easily understand the difference between time periods, they are improving their temporal orientation.

7. **Metaphorical thinking** is being able to emphasize similarities between two unrelated or indirectly linked things. The metaphor is not only an important literary tool but also a way to encourage learners to be creative in whatever subject they are studying. With practice in creating and discovering metaphors, learners improve their thinking.

8. **Spiritual dimensions** encompass a learner's ability to sense emotional, spiritual, or intuitive communication. Beliefs, feelings, and values directly affect all aspects of our lives, including the teaching/learning transaction. What learners believe and feel about themselves, the subject matter, and learning in general directly impacts their cognitive development.

Suggestions to increase cognitive structures in learners include the following.

- Work on relationships. When learners have a higher level of trust, they will open up more often and explain when they are struggling to make an idea fit in their mind.

- Encourage learners to reflect, not just jump to conclusions. Ask them to suspend judgment as they focus on making as many observations as possible.

- Urge learners to use their imagination and mental manipulations and to think creatively. Help learners make sense of observations and information.

- Maximize lessons by designing instruction that allows learners to discover answers and solutions on their own.

- Use open-ended questions, frequently asking learners to make comparisons and predictions and to give explanations.

Social Skills

The lack of certain social skills can become significant barriers to learning and learner engagement. Social skills include such behaviors as greeting others, accepting compliments, handling criticism, negotiating, and working as a group. Teachers should be alert to learners' lack of social skills and should post the behaviors that are expected of learners, reinforce the proper use of skills, and work with them to correct poor behavior. Teaching learners how to get along with their peers, school staff, and family members is becoming an increasingly important role of the educator. Contemporary research has shown that developing social skills is critical to learners' academic and personal successes. The A. J. Moore Academy, a high school in Waco, Texas, has an excellent list of the social skills that are deliberately taught, reinforced, and practiced throughout the school.

Classroom Social Skills

Changing Classes

- Exit the room in an orderly way.
- Get the materials for the next class.
- Walk quickly to class, using low voice tones.
- Keep hands, feet, and other body parts to yourself.
- Greet the teacher and enter the room before the tardy bell rings.

Beginning Class

- Enter the room in an orderly way.
- Sit in your assigned seat immediately.
- Have your materials ready.
- Begin the focus activity.
- Wait quietly for further instructions.

Taking a Test

- Prepare the materials.
- Listen to directions.
- Work quietly.
- Do your own work.
- Stay seated and don't violate others' space.

Completing Work

- Turn your work into the tray quietly.
- Return to your seat quietly.
- Read your Accelerated Reader book quietly.

Ending Class

- When the bell rings, wait for the teacher to dismiss you.
- Get up slowly.
- Push your chair in and clean up the area.
- Walk out in an orderly manner.

Going to and from Lunch

- Keep moving. Walk and talk in low tones.
- Keep hands, feet, and other body parts to yourself.
- Arrive at lunch on time. Stay in the cafeteria until lunch is over.
- Stay out of classrooms that are not at lunch.

Following Instructions

- Look at the person.
- Say "okay."
- Do what you've been asked right away.
- Check back.
- Raise your hand and wait to be acknowledged for questions and for collecting tests.

Accepting Criticism or a Consequence

- Look at the person.
- Say "okay."
- Don't argue.

Accepting "No" for an Answer

- Look at the person.
- Say "okay."
- Stay calm.
- If you disagree, ask later.

Disagreeing Appropriately

- Look at the person.
- Use a pleasant voice.
- Say, "I understand how you feel."
- Tell why you feel differently.
- Give a reason.

Greeting Others

- Look at the person.
- Use a pleasant voice.
- Say "hi" or "hello."
- Listen to the other person.

Giving Criticism

- Look at the person.
- Stay calm. Use a pleasant voice.
- Say something positive or "I understand."
- Describe exactly what you are criticizing.
- Tell why this is a problem.
- Listen to the person. Be polite.

Getting the Teacher's Attention

- Look at the teacher.
- Raise your hand. Stay calm.
- Wait until the teacher says your name.
- Ask your question.

Making a Request

- Look at the person.
- Use a clear, pleasant voice.
- Explain exactly what you are asking for. Say "please."
- If the answer is "yes," say "thank you."
- If not, remember to accept "no" for an answer.

Resisting Peer Pressure

- Look at the person.
- Use a calm voice.
- Say clearly that you do not want to participate.
- Suggest something else to do.
- If necessary, continue to say "no."
- Leave the situation.

Making an Apology

- Look at the person.
- Use a serious, sincere voice.
- Say, "I'm sorry for . . . " or "I want to apologize for . . ."
- Do not make excuses.
- Explain how you plan to do better in the future.
- Say, "Thanks for listening."

Talking with Others

- Look at the person.
- Use a pleasant voice.
- Ask questions.
- Don't interrupt.

Giving Compliments

- Look at the person.
- Smile.
- Speak clearly and enthusiastically.
- Tell the person exactly what you like.

Accepting Compliments

- Look at the person.
- Say "thank you."
- Don't look away, mumble, or deny the compliment.
- Do not disagree with the compliment.

Volunteering

- Look at the person.
- Use a pleasant, enthusiastic voice.
- Ask if you can help.
- Describe the activity or task that you are offering to do.
- Thank the person.
- Check back when you have finished.

Reporting Other Youths' Behavior

- Look at the teacher or the adult.
- Use a calm voice. Ask to talk to him/her privately.
- Describe the inappropriate behavior you are reporting.
- Explain why you are making the report.
- Answer any questions the adult has.
- Thank the adult for listening.

Introducing Yourself

- Look at the person. Smile.
- Use a pleasant voice.
- Offer a greeting. Say, "Hi, my name is. . . ."
- Shake the person's hand.
- When you leave, say, "It was nice to meet you."

Social-Emotional Learning Standards

A number of states, provinces, and districts have developed social-emotional learning standards and benchmarks. Standards have been developed both as distinct stand-alone content areas and as subsections of health, language arts, career education, and other subjects. The following example of such standards comes from the Illinois State Board of Education. British Columbia, New Jersey, Ohio, and Wisconsin have developed similar standards that draw increased attention to social-emotional learning. Does your school have clear standards for social-emotional learning?

Illinois Social-Emotional Learning Standards

GOAL 1: Develop self-awareness and self-management skills to achieve school and life success.

1. Identify and manage one's own emotions and behavior.
2. Recognize personal qualities and external supports.
3. Demonstrate skills related to achieving personal and academic goals.

GOAL 2: Use social awareness and interpersonal skills to establish and maintain positive relationships.

1. Recognize the feelings and perspectives of others.
2. Recognize the individual and group similarities and differences.
3. Use communication and social skills to interact effectively with others.
4. Demonstrate an ability to prevent, manage, and resolve interpersonal conflicts in constructive ways.

GOAL 3: Demonstrate decision-making skills and responsible behaviors in personal, school, and community contexts.

1. Consider ethical, safety, and societal factors in making decisions.
2. Apply decision-making skills to deal responsibly with daily academic and social situations.
3. Contribute to the well-being of one's school and community.

Fundamental Skills Self-Check

Always	Sometimes	Rarely	
☐	☐	☐	1. I reinforce with learners effective planning/organizational skills to complete in-class tasks and homework.
☐	☐	☐	2. I reinforce with learners procedures for taking notes and recording key information for future reference.
☐	☐	☐	3. Learners have learned techniques for memorizing information.
☐	☐	☐	4. Learners practice communication skills appropriate to the goals of the class.
☐	☐	☐	5. Learners practice active listening (such as body posture, giving feedback, asking questions, and summarizing).
☐	☐	☐	6. Learners can stay on task and work independently.
☐	☐	☐	7. Learners use questioning skills effectively.
☐	☐	☐	8. I model and practice social skills (such as interrupting politely, active listening, constructive feedback, and respectful communication).
☐	☐	☐	9. Learners use coaching effectively when working with peers.
☐	☐	☐	10. I pay attention to the thinking processes of learners and the cognitive structures they use to solve problems.
☐	☐	☐	11. I give learners feedback and encourage them to reflect on their work.
☐	☐	☐	12. I reinforce with learners how to work cooperatively in small groups.
☐	☐	☐	13. I reinforce with learners how to use appropriate social skills (greeting guests, responding to adults and peers, entering conversations, accepting compliments/criticism).
☐	☐	☐	14. Learners use appropriate skills to resolve conflicts and negotiate compromises.

 **Chapter 6**

Engagement-Based Learning and Teaching — Pedagogy

Introduction

Pedagogy is the second element that constitutes engagement-based learning and teaching (EBLT). *Pedagogy* is defined as "the activities of teaching."

Chapter 5 describes the preconditions for teaching. Each of these preconditions has aspects that carry over into teaching. However, the preconditions, which relate to the planning and preparation for teaching, are primarily the responsibility of the entire school community. The preconditions help make it possible for teachers to have highly engaged learners. Preconditions might be considered necessary — but they, alone, are not sufficient.

It is pedagogy (more specifically, effective pedagogy) that leads to high levels of engagement. Preconditions make it possible, and pedagogy makes it happen! Pedagogy is the responsibility of the teacher working with individual groups of learners. To achieve engagement-based learning and teaching, teachers must reflect on their pedagogical practices as well as develop and implement additional practices that increase learner engagement.

The following factors of pedagogy help teachers create rigorous and relevant learning.

1. designing for rigorous and relevant learning
2. personalized learning
3. active learning strategies
4. focus on reading

Designing for Rigorous and Relevant Learning — Tips and Techniques

> Relevance makes rigor possible.
>
> — *Willard Daggett, Chairman and Founder, ICLE*

One of the barriers to high levels of learner engagement is the lack of rigorous and relevant instruction. While it is essential that learners acquire basic skills before they proceed to more complex work, teachers should not keep learners hostage by implying that they must complete all the isolated basics before they have the opportunity to engage in challenging and applied learning experiences. Relevance is just as critical as rigor. Relevance can help create the conditions and motivation necessary for learners to make the personal investment required for rigorous work or optimal learning. Learners invest more of themselves, work harder, and learn better when the topic is interesting and connected to something that they already know.

A growing trend in describing school improvement is to aspire for rigor and relevance. The challenge for teachers is to translate this aspiration into classroom practice.

Defining Rigor

Rigor refers to academic rigor — learning in which learners demonstrate a thorough, in-depth mastery of challenging tasks that develop cognitive skills through reflective thought, analysis, problem-solving, evaluation, or creativity. Rigorous learning can occur at any school grade and in any subject. Doing more and longer assignments does not equal rigor. Rigor is about the quality, not the quantity, of learner work.

Defining Relevance

Relevance refers to learning in which learners apply core knowledge, concepts, or skills to solve real-world problems. Relevant learning is interdisciplinary and contextual. Learner work can range from routine to complex at any school grade and in any subject. Relevant learning is created, for example, through authentic problems or tasks, simulation, service learning, connecting concepts to current issues, and teaching others.

Rigor/Relevance Framework

The Rigor/Relevance Framework® is a tool developed by the International Center for Leadership in Education to examine curriculum, instruction, and assessment. With this tool, teachers can quantify the levels of rigor and relevance in learner learning and can make adjustments to increase rigor and relevance over time.

In 2001 Bloom's Knowledge Taxonomy was updated and revised by Lorin Anderson, a student of Bloom's, and David Krathwohl, a colleague, to reflect the movement to standards-based curricula and assessment. Nouns in Bloom's original model were changed to verb forms (for example, *knowledge* to *remembering* and *comprehension* to *understanding*) and slightly reordered. We believe that the original Bloom's taxonomy as shown in our Rigor/Relevance Framework clearly describes expectations for Quadrants A, B, C, and D. The revised Bloom's elevates the importance of Quadrants B and D and indicates how 21st-century lessons should be built. We regard both the original and revised taxonomies as necessary and important.

The Rigor/Relevance Framework is based on two dimensions of higher standards and learner achievement.

First, there is a continuum of knowledge that describes the increasingly complex ways in which we think. The Knowledge Taxonomy, which describes the levels of rigor, is based on the six levels of Bloom's Taxonomy: (1) knowledge/awareness, (2) comprehension, (3) application, (4) analysis, (5) synthesis, and (6) evaluation. An excellent practice is to select verbs synonymous with each of the six levels when setting the level of thinking you want learners to achieve.

The second dimension is the Application Model, which describes the levels of relevance and the increasingly complex applications of knowledge and skills. Any learner performance can be expressed as one of five levels of the Application Model:

> Level 1 — Knowledge in One Discipline
>
> Level 2 — Application in One Discipline
>
> Level 3 — Interdisciplinary Application
>
> Level 4 — Real-World Predictable Situations
>
> Level 5 — Real-World Unpredictable Situations

The low end of this continuum involves acquiring knowledge and being able to recall or locate that knowledge in a simple manner. Just as a computer completes a word search in a word processing program, a competent person at this level can scan through thousands of bits of information in the brain to locate that desired knowledge. The high end of the Knowledge Taxonomy labels more complex ways in which individuals use knowledge. At this level, knowledge is fully integrated into one's mind, and individuals can do much more than recall information: They can take several pieces of knowledge and combine them in both logical and creative ways. Assimilation of knowledge is a good way to describe this high level of the thinking continuum. Assimilation is often referred to as a higher-order thinking skill; at this level, the learner can solve multistep problems and create unique work and solutions. The Rigor/Relevance Framework is the relational connection between these two scales.

The Framework has four quadrants: A, B, C, and D.

Quadrant A — Acquisition. Learners gather and store bits of knowledge and information. Learners primarily are expected to understand and remember this acquired knowledge.

Quadrant B — Application. Learners use acquired knowledge to solve problems, design solutions, and complete work. The highest level of application is to apply appropriate knowledge to new and unpredictable situations.

Quadrant C — Assimilation. Learners extend and refine their acquired knowledge so that they can use that knowledge automatically and routinely to analyze and solve problems and create unique solutions.

Quadrant D — Adaptation. Learners have the competence to think in complex ways and to apply knowledge and skills that they have acquired. Even when confronted with perplexing unknowns, learners are able to use their extensive knowledge and skill to create solutions and take action that further develops their skills and knowledge.

Quadrant A represents simple recall and basic understanding of knowledge for its own sake. Quadrant C represents more complex thinking but still knowledge for its own sake. Examples of Quadrant A knowledge are knowing that the world is round and that Shakespeare wrote *Hamlet*. Quadrant C embraces higher levels of knowledge, such as knowing how the U.S. political system works and analyzing the benefits and challenges of the cultural diversity of this nation versus other nations.

Quadrants B and D represent action or high degrees of application. Quadrant B would include knowing how to use math skills to make purchases and count change. The ability to access information in wide-area network systems and the ability to gather knowledge from a variety of sources to solve a complex problem in the workplace are types of Quadrant D knowledge. Each of these four quadrants can also be labeled with a term that characterizes the learning or learner performance.

Rigor/Relevance Framework®

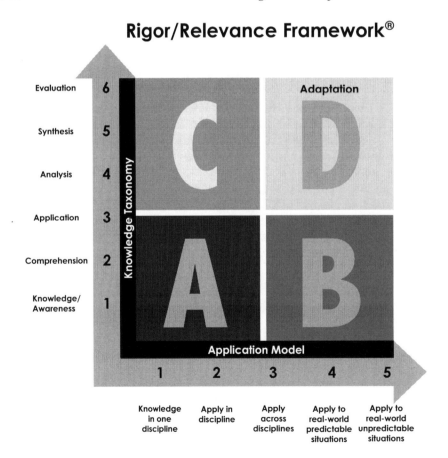

© International Center for Leadership in Education

Knowledge Taxonomy Verb List

Quadrant A	Quadrant B	Quadrant C	Quadrant D
calculate	adjust	analyze	adapt
choose	apply	categorize	compose
count	build	classify	conclude
define	collect	compare	create
describe	construct	conclude	design
find	demonstrate	contrast	develop
identify	display	debate	discover
label	dramatize	defend	explore
list	draw	diagram	formulate
locate	fix	differentiate	invent
match	follow	discriminate	modify
memorize	illustrate	evaluate	plan
name	interpret	examine	predict
point to	interview	explain	prioritize
recall	look up	express	propose
recite	maintain	generate	rate
record	make	infer	recommend
say	measure	judge	revise
select	model	justify	teach
spell	operate	prove	
view	play	research	
	practice	study	
	produce	summarize	
	relate		
	role play		
	sequence		
	show		
	solve		
	tune		
	use		

The following example of learner performance applies each quadrant to technical reading and writing.

Quadrant A: Define vocabulary terms needed to understand content of a classroom simulation.

Quadrant B: Complete a simulation following the directions given by the instructor.

Quadrant C: Compare and contrast the information gained from two simulations with that gained from reading a text on the same topic.

Quadrant D: Synthesize information from a range of sources (e.g., texts, media sources, simulations), presenting solutions to conflicting information.

Teaching and Learning in the Rigor/Relevance Framework

An example of learner performance at various levels of the Knowledge Taxonomy follows. Notice that each statement starts with a verb that parallels the Knowledge Taxonomy. The expected achievement level for teaching about nutrition can vary depending on the purpose of the instruction. If a teacher wants learners only to acquire basic nutritional knowledge, a learner performance set at Level 1 or 2 is adequate. If the instruction is intended to have a more significant impact on nutritional habits, then some of the objectives need to be similar to levels 4–6.

Note that each level requires learners to think differently. Levels 4–6 require more complex thinking than do levels 1–3. When creating lesson plans and learner objectives, selecting the proper verb can help to describe the appropriate performance. Simply start with a verb for the desired level and finish the statement with a specific description of that skill or knowledge area.

Basic Nutrition

Level 1 — Knowledge	1. Label foods by nutritional groups.
Level 2 — Comprehension	2. Explain the nutritional value of individual foods.
Level 3 — Application	3. Make use of nutrition guidelines in planning meals.
Level 4 — Analysis	4. Examine successes in achieving nutrition goals.
Level 5 — Synthesis	5. Develop personal nutrition goals.
Level 6 — Evaluation	6. Appraise results of personal eating habits over time.

The Application Model of the Rigor/Relevance Framework describes putting knowledge to use. While the low end is knowledge acquired for its own sake, the high end signifies action — use of that knowledge to solve complex real-world problems and to create projects, designs, and other works for use in real-world situations.

Basic Nutrition

Level 1 — Knowledge in One Discipline	1. Label foods by nutritional groups.
Level 2 — Application in One Discipline	2. Rank foods by nutritional value.
Level 3 — Interdisciplinary Application	3. Make cost comparisons of different foods, considering their nutritional value.
Level 4 — Real-World Predictable Situations	4. Develop a nutritional plan for a person with a health problem that is affected by food intake.
Level 5 — Real-World Unpredictable Situations	5. Devise a sound nutritional plan for 3-year-olds who are picky eaters.

Teacher/Learner Roles

> We learn by example and by direct experience because there are real limits to the adequacy of verbal instruction.
>
> — *Malcolm Gladwell, author*

One way to think about the Rigor/Relevance Framework in day-to-day instruction is in terms of the roles that teachers and learners take in the classroom. These roles are represented in the following figure.

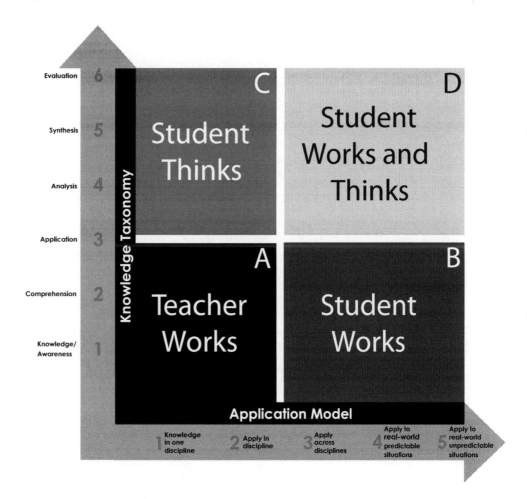

When instruction and expected learning is in Quadrant A, the focus is on "teacher work." Teachers expend energy to create and assess learning activities through providing information, creating worksheets, and grading learner work. The learner often is a passive learner. When the learner expectation moves to Quadrant B, the emphasis is on the learner's doing real-world work. This learner work is often more complicated than Quadrant A work and requires more time. Learning in Quadrant B is best described as "learner work" because learners are doing extensive real-world tasks.

When the learning is placed in Quadrant C, it is best described as "learner think." In this quadrant, learners are expected to think in complex ways — to analyze, compare, create, and evaluate. The term that best describes Quadrant D activities is "learner think and work." Learning in Quadrant D is more demanding and requires the learner to think and work. Roles shift from the teacher-centered instruction in Quadrant A to learner-centered instruction in Quadrants B, C, and D. Teachers still work in Quadrants B, C, and D, but their role is more as a coach or facilitator.

Learner Answers

Another way to distinguish learning among the four quadrants is by looking at whether the learners "got it right" in terms of how the work will be evaluated. When

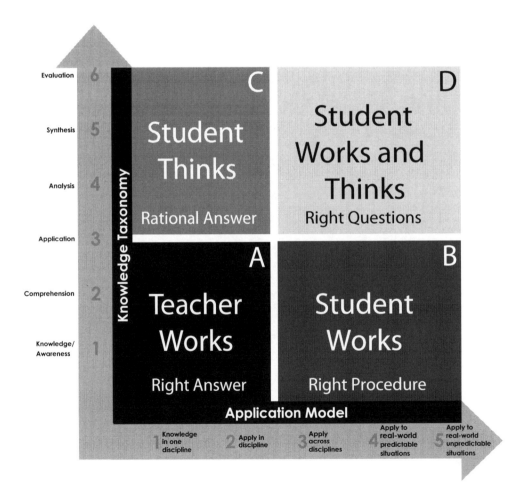

instruction is in Quadrant A, there is clearly a right answer. When the level of learning moves up into Quadrant C, often there is more than one right answer, and the teacher is looking for original work that reflects logical and rational thinking on the learner's part. Quadrant C is about rational answers. With real-world learning in Quadrant B, instruction often involves having the learner follow a procedure to do some work, and the right answer requires doing the procedure correctly. In Quadrant D, the learner is working on complex real-world problems, and results depend upon whether the learner asked all the right questions in order to consider everything that should have been included in solving the problem.

Strategies for Teaching for Rigor and Relevance

- Use a "backward design" approach: Start with where you want learners to end up. How will learners demonstrate that they have learned the skills and knowledge? What level of rigor and relevance do you expect? Once you have decided the end goal, work backward to determine how to take learners from their current knowledge and skill levels to reach your objective. *Rigor and relevance always should be a forethought, not an afterthought, in planning.*

- It takes more time to teach in Quadrant D for high rigor/high relevance. Start with the most important concepts in your subject at your grade level. What do you want learners to learn "deeply" and retain beyond your class? This is the lesson you should be teaching in Quadrant D.

- Teach and test at the same level. In order for learners to learn at higher levels, testing must be at the same level of rigor and relevance as teaching. Teachers who assign an interesting project but end up testing and grading learners on basic vocabulary words, for example, are not teaching to high levels of rigor and relevance. Make sure that assessment procedures match the level of rigor and relevance that you expect learners to have acquired.

- All four quadrants of the Framework are important. When introducing activities that call for higher degrees of application, make sure learners understand that this work is as important as acquiring knowledge. Likewise, learner work that requires higher-level thinking skills should be required of all learners, not as optional work for more advanced learners.

- There is no standard answer to the question "How often should I be teaching in Quadrant D?" However, teachers should constantly look for opportunities to raise the levels of rigor and relevance. Sometimes simply asking a more reflective question or selecting a real-world application will challenge learners in daily instruction. Some elementary teachers develop a routine of a major interdisciplinary project each month for their class and one each semester for the group of classes in the same grade level. Some high school teachers with courses that have high-stakes, content-based tests use one major Quadrant D project at the end of the year. Teachers of other high school subjects tend to have each unit of instruction culminate with a Quadrant D presentation. Models of teaching to high rigor/high relevance will vary, but teachers always should be seeking opportunities.

- Don't hold learners hostage in Quadrant A. While it is important to learn basic content, some learners will not stay engaged in learning long enough to acquire the skills they need. For these learners, a better instructional sequence is to start with an engaging real-world problem. When learners realize that they don't have all the knowledge or skills to create a solution, help them acquire Quadrant A learning. More learners will become engaged and successful by changing the sequence of instruction.

- Learn from other teachers. When you share sample Quadrant D lessons across a school, you can learn from others. Even if a teacher works with a different grade level or teaches another subject, you can focus on the characteristics of rigor and relevance that make it a good lesson. This strategy may stimulate ideas for you about how to add rigor and relevance to what you teach.

- High rigor/high relevance lessons are naturally interdisciplinary. As you create these lessons, be open to incorporating other disciplines. To make your lessons even better, consult with other teachers on staff who have more expertise.

Design for Rigor/Relevance Self-Check

Always	Sometimes	Rarely	
☐	☐	☐	1. My instruction is well planned and prepared in advance.
☐	☐	☐	2. My instruction has clear expectations for levels of rigor and relevance using the Rigor/Relevance Framework.
☐	☐	☐	3. My instruction is built with the goal of culminating in a performance task.
☐	☐	☐	4. My instruction is planned using data about learners' prior experiences and achievement levels.
☐	☐	☐	5. My instruction informs learners of the expected performance, essential questions, and assessment criteria at the beginning of the lesson or unit.
☐	☐	☐	6. I show learners' work samples that exemplify proficient/nonproficient levels of performance.
☐	☐	☐	7. My instruction is guided by "big ideas" (abstract concepts) and essential questions.
☐	☐	☐	8. My instruction includes teaching the knowledge and skills necessary for expected learner performance.

Design for Rigor/Relevance Self-Check (Continued)

☐	☐	☐	9. My instruction calls for learners to demonstrate their understanding of knowledge and skills by applying what they have learned in activities and tasks.
☐	☐	☐	10. My instruction calls for learners to demonstrate their understanding of knowledge and skills by applying what they have learned in activities and tasks.
☐	☐	☐	11. My instruction uses a variety of teaching resources.
☐	☐	☐	12. I use the textbook as only one resource among many.
☐	☐	☐	13. My instruction is linked to priority state standards.
☐	☐	☐	14. My instruction assesses standard(s) at the appropriate level of rigor.
☐	☐	☐	15. My instruction uses authentic assessments.
☐	☐	☐	16. My instruction uses clear evaluation criteria and performance standards.
☐	☐	☐	17. My instruction uses information from ongoing assessments to analyze learning and to dispel misconceptions along the way.
☐	☐	☐	18. My instruction uses rubrics/scoring guides to delineate levels of proficiency.

Personalized Learning — Tips and Techniques

> Many children struggle in schools . . . because the way they are being taught is incompatible with the way they learn.
>
> — *Peter Senge, MIT Sloan School of Management*

Each learner brings a unique set of characteristics to the classroom. Each one has different background knowledge, a unique learning style, a variety of interests, and varied levels of parental support and expectations. To anticipate that all learners will learn in the same way, at the same speed, and through the same material is an unrealistic expectation.

Some teachers assume that the learner is at fault when he/she fails to demonstrate adequate achievement. However, it often is the lack of personalized learning that is the source of failure. There are many individual practices and strategies that contribute to overall personalization. As a start, teachers can create a more engaging classroom situation by getting to know their learners and by using examples during instruction that relate to their backgrounds, cultures, and prior experiences. Parent involvement also is a part of personalizing learning. By reaching out to parents and establishing cooperation and support for learning expectations, teachers are able to achieve greater personalization.

Learners also need to experience differentiated instruction that is not constantly based on large-group instruction that moves at the same rate of speed. There should be opportunities and challenges for them to do individual assignments and to work at their own speed — to move more slowly on more difficult material and more quickly on concepts or skills in which they have higher proficiency levels.

Strategies for Personalizing Learning

> Every learner can learn, just not on the same day, or the same way.
>
> — *George Evans*

Personalizing learning involves using a set of instructional strategies and approaches that take into account the uniqueness of each learner. Teachers may be committed to common learning goals, but getting every learner to achieve those goals requires personalizing the process. Strategies to do so include:

- Make each learner feel unique.
- Connect to the youth culture.
- Recognize cultural differences.
- Consider the learner's point of view.
- Be aware of different learning styles.
- Build self-confidence through learner efficacy.
- Differentiate instruction.
- Attend to learners with special needs.
- Intervene early.

Each of these strategies is discussed in more detail on the following pages.

Make Each Learner Feel Unique

- Techniques such as making eye contact, maintaining proximity, calling learners by name, and using positive personal examples that learners can relate to are all good ways to make learners feel special.
- Give individual attention to each learner by having short conferences. While learners are working at their desks, walk around the room. Stop by each desk and whisper a comment to the learner about the work that he/she is doing.

- When learners are absent, tell them that you missed them; make them feel that they are an important part of the class. If a learner is absent because of a long illness, have the class write get-well messages and mail them. If a learner experiences a death in the family, teach the class how to write sympathy notes.

- Try to give learners choices, and respect the choices they make. For instance, give a general assignment such as sharing a memorable childhood experience. Then, help learners brainstorm ways in which they can handle the assignment individually — through writing, using visuals, and so on.

- Sometimes allow learners to choose their own reading material within guidelines that you set. Learners are more invested in their own learning if they are given opportunities to make choices.

Connect to the Youth Culture

One effective way of raising engagement in any subject is to incorporate youth culture in the classroom. Music, television, advertising, sports, Internet chat, celebrities, friends, clothes, family, and neighborhood conditions are all strong influences. Hip-hop, for example, has become a defining social movement of today's generation. A generation of youth — urban, rural, racially diverse, poor, and rich — define themselves according to their pop culture idols. One difference today is that ubiquitous and instantaneous media make counterculture more visible than in any previous generation. Teachers, however, can use pop culture as a tool to turn learning into a more engaging experience. For example, learners could create a rap song to learn vocabulary words or compare lyrics of a popular song to a theme in classic literature.

Recognize Cultural Differences

- Use "cultural relevancy" tactics to engage minority learners in order to help them do better in school. An example of "getting it wrong" occurred when an inner-city math teacher tried to explain the geometrical concept of a slope by using ski terminology. Another inner-city middle school math teacher did better working with learners on the subject of ratios and proportions. This teacher asked learners to record the number of alcohol billboards and liquor stores they passed on their way to school and calculate the number of each per block. This was their cultural knowledge. (The National Urban Alliance maintains an extensive list of resources to assist teachers in adding culturally appropriate learning experiences.)

- Design some lessons and activities that incorporate strong African-American or Hispanic cultural values of community and teamwork and the contrast with individualism and competition as primary strategies for success. Be willing to discuss issues concerning gender/racial bias, discrimination, racial profiling, and the like, taking a stand for social justice.

- Create a multicultural atmosphere in the classroom. Display pictures of all racial groups, as well as learners with disabilities. Remember to balance the genders. Get to know your learners, their communities, and their cultures. Make connections and celebrate the diversity of backgrounds.

Consider the Learner's Point of View

> The best learners . . . often make the worst teach-
> ers. They are, in a very real sense, perceptually chal-
> lenged. They cannot imagine what it must be like to
> struggle to learn something that comes so naturally
> to them.
>
> *— Stephen Brookfield, internationally*
> *acclaimed scholar in adult education*

- Good teachers know their content areas deeply and thoroughly. Your role is to help learners acquire appropriate knowledge in a particular subject. To do that effectively, you need to look at your content area, based not on what you know but on what the learner knows.

- Give learners the opportunity to construct learning by developing their own links to new knowledge through self-discovery. Just as our ancestors explored their world and learned what items were edible and where danger existed, so too can learners explore their world through carefully designed instruction. For example, a math teacher using the naming strategy to teach about associative properties typically gives learners the term, defines it, and gives examples in symbols: $x = a(bc)$ is equivalent to $x = (ab)c$. A constructivist approach, in contrast, might start with learners solving a two-digit multiplication problem in their heads. After learners explain how they arrived at the answer, the teacher would note that not all learners followed the same sequence of steps, yet each arrived at the correct answer. After learners discover that numbers can be multiplied in any sequence, the teacher can label this the commutative process. Learners will retain the links to this new knowledge because it has been constructed largely from their own experience.

- A personalized teaching strategy might be to start a class with inquiry-based instruction instead of reading long passages or terms to memorize. Start with observations. This creates a more personalized approach, in which learners are more engaged in active learning as they move into the heart of a lesson.

Be Aware of Different Learning Styles

Another aspect of personalizing learning is recognizing the learning styles of learners. Understanding the different ways that learners learn, interact with, and process information can help teachers modify instructional strategies so that all learners have an opportunity to succeed. The learning styles theory is rooted in the classification of psychological types; it is based on research that has shown that as the result of heredity, upbringing, and environment, different individuals have a tendency to perceive and process information differently. There are many learning style theory models, which all have some validity. The most common model incorporates three learning styles: visual, auditory, and kinesthetic.

Visual Learners

- need to see it to know it
- have a strong sense of color

- may have artistic ability
- may have difficulty with oral directions
- may overreact to sounds
- may have trouble following lectures
- may misinterpret words

Auditory Learners

- need to hear it to know it
- do better following oral directions
- may have difficulty with reading and/or writing
- may have trouble reading body language and facial expressions
- are more effective at giving oral presentations

Kinesthetic Learners

- prefer hands-on learning
- often can assemble parts without reading directions
- have difficulty sitting still
- learn better when physical activity is involved
- may be well coordinated

Teachers should design instruction to connect with all learning styles, using various combinations of experience, conceptualization, experimentation, and reflection. Varying teaching strategies ensures that learners will learn in a manner compatible with their own learning preferences. It also expands the repertoire of learning strategies experienced by the entire class. By surveying learners and building an inventory of interests, teachers can obtain a better sense about how to modify instruction and activities to enhance their learners' interests.

Build Self-Confidence Through Learner Efficacy

> We should spend less time ranking children and more time helping them to identify their natural competencies and gifts and cultivate these. There are hundreds and hundreds of ways to succeed and many, many different abilities that will help you get there.
>
> — *Howard Gardner, known for his theory of multiple intelligences*

Learner efficacy means that learners realize their potential as learners. Many learners do not become engaged in learning because they are afraid of failure and lack the confidence to identify themselves as "good learners." The Efficacy Institute's model for efficacy is a developmental process that informs learners that academic achievement is not something that is fixed at birth or by socioeconomic or cultural factors.

"Smart is not something you are. Smart is something you get," says Jeff Howard, founder of The Efficacy Institute.

The efficacy model states that confidence leads to effective effort, which then leads to achievement. When teachers talk about effective effort, they are talking about commitment to study for long periods of time, from elementary school through college. It requires some teachers to shift their paradigm to see children in a different way, by expecting them to come to school ready and able to learn. To allow learners to obtain self-efficacy, teachers must build learners' confidence and inspire them to commit the necessary effort. That effort leads to real achievement. When young people confront difficulty, teachers should not give any indication that they are judging learners' abilities. Instead, teachers should model excitement and determination about "figuring out what the problem is." Teachers are encouraged to create classroom and community environments in which young people respond to failure or difficulty with vigor. Teach them that their success depends on the level and quality of their effort.

Differentiate Instruction

To understand what differentiation is, understand first what it is not. Differentiation is not planning individual lessons for each learner every day. It is not teaching to the middle group and giving more work to accelerated learners and less work to underachieving learners. Finally, differentiation is not placing learners in cooperative learning structures and failing to hold them accountable for individual roles and achievement.

In assigning learners to cooperative learning groups, think about engaging each learner in an individual role based on his or her knowledge, learning style, and interests that contribute to group learning. Differentiated instruction requires teachers to be flexible in their approach to teaching and to adjust the curriculum to learner needs rather than expecting the learners to adapt themselves to the curriculum. Here are some suggestions to enhance differentiated instruction.

- **Differentiate the content.** Pretest learners to identify those who require direct instruction and those who can move quickly to apply the concept/knowledge/skill. This preassessment should provide a clear representation of knowledge and skills by entailing more than a litany of facts. It should measure what the learner knows, understands, and is able to do.

- **Differentiate the teaching process and activities**. Vary learning activities or instructional strategies to provide alternative methods for learners to explore the concepts.

- **Differentiate the product.** Vary the types of results that learners must produce to demonstrate mastery of the concept.

- **Differentiate by manipulating the environment to accommodate individual learning styles.** Change the lighting or sound levels, eliminate visual distractions, and/or provide a more casual seating arrangement for learners. Vary teaching strategies to ensure that learners have opportunities to learn in a manner compatible with their learning preference.

Attend to Learners with Special Needs

Often, the group experiencing the most serious gap in educational performance has been learners with disabilities. While many plausible explanations for the size of this performance gap are offered, there also is a growing recognition that it should not be as wide as it is. One aspect of personalizing learning is making sure that in the course of classroom instruction, the unique learning needs of learners with disabilities are addressed.

The International Center believes that:

- all children can learn
- not every child with a disability can meet general education standards, but most can
- more learners with disabilities can meet standards than we have expected
- many more learners with disabilities can meet standards than have so far
- the expectations of the education system for these learners are too low

Many general and special educators were trained when schools had low expectations of the potential of learners receiving special education services. Furthermore, the world in which today's learners will live has changed dramatically. As understanding of these realities increases, it will reinforce why schools must improve performance to give learners with disabilities greater opportunities to reach the vision that the laws have set out for them.

Following are some strategies that teachers can use in meeting the needs of learners with disabilities.

- The general education teacher should be the first line of support for learners with disabilities. Ownership of learner progress by these teachers is essential.
- Develop a culture of achievement, regardless of learners' ability levels.
- Arrange ongoing, explicit discussions with learners, parents, other teachers, guidance counselors, and administrators regarding high expectations for academic performance.
- Special education teachers should arrange for additional time on tasks in courses that are challenging for learners with disabilities and should plan instructional sessions before and after school with general education teachers to learn content and skills.
- Expect learners to be engaged independently after school hours with assignments and studying.
- Develop a method that uses planners and notebooks to assist learners with the organization of their program/courses.
- Create study guides for learners. This task should be a shared responsibility of general education and special education teachers.
- Teach learners to develop their own study guides for unit exams. This process will enable them to prioritize and organize information independently.

Intervene Early

Reaching the goal of having all learners succeed requires several levels of intervention, and early intervention is key. These levels of intervention are components of personalizing learning. Teachers must monitor learner progress frequently with formal and informal assessments and then use this information to help them decide what to teach. Share assessment results with learners, parents, and tutors.

Possible academic interventions early in the school year include:

- three-week academic progress reports mailed to all parents
- extracurricular coaches and advisors who serve as academic support
- monitoring academic success on a regular basis
- quarterly academic improvement awards granted to learners
- a special effort to make one positive telephone call each quarter to the parents of these learners, who might never have received a phone call from school bearing good news
- tutoring during lunch, before or after school by teachers, upper-class learners, parent volunteers, retired teachers, and the like
- Saturday literacy improvement classes
- a meeting between an entire grade-level team and individual learners to work as a group to address achievement issues
- special preparation sessions for state tests

Although teachers should use positive reinforcement when engaging learners, when complimenting their work, the feedback should be focused and specific. Providing feedback that is "great job" doesn't provide enough detail for the learner as to *what* was great. Taking the time to provide more targeted feedback will help to engage learners in a deeper way. Here are some examples of what to say and what not to say:

Ways Not to Compliment Learners' Work	Ways to Compliment Learners' Work
• Awesome! • Great! • Nice job! • I like that! • Super job! • That's right! • Good work! • Well done! • Way to go! • You are learning fast!	• I like how you used a visual to express your thinking. • Your work is very organized and clear. • Great job with taking the time to solve the problem. • I like how you used evidence from the text to support your thinking. • I like how you used data to supporting your thinking. • Great job with using multiple sources to support your thinking. • I like how you made the activity relevant to your personal life. • Your persistence in solving the problem is something you should be proud of. • I like how you provided an opportunity for others in your group to share their thinking. • I like how you included what you learned in science class to math class. • I can see how your creative thinking came through in your use of graphics. • I like how you challenged yourself to take the activity to the next level. • I like how you worked well with others. • You asked relevant questions about the learning today. • Your writing includes great detail. • I like how you showed your work when solving the problem. • I like how you showed multiple ways to solve the problem. • I like how you used technology as a resource for learning. • I like how you brought ideas from the community to the classroom. • I like how you took a leadership role in your learning team. • You synthesized the information to develop an original solution. • You did a great job in evaluating your own work to make it better. • You are confident when sharing your ideas. • You are committed to the learning. • I can tell you take great pride in your work. • You did a great job citing multiple sources.

Personalization Self-Check

Always	Sometimes	Rarely	
☐	☐	☐	1. I have high expectations for all learners to achieve expected performance goals.
☐	☐	☐	2. I use a variety of instructional strategies that match the varied learning styles of my learners.
☐	☐	☐	3. Learners have opportunities to demonstrate their talents during the learning experience.
☐	☐	☐	4. Learners have an advocate, such as a teacher, principal, or guidance counselor, to whom they can talk about school issues.
☐	☐	☐	5. Learners with disabilities are provided opportunities for full participation in the curriculum.
☐	☐	☐	6. Appropriate accommodations are provided for learners with learning disabilities.
☐	☐	☐	7. I frequently confer with individual learners about their academic progress.
☐	☐	☐	8. I adjust instruction based on learner reflection and feedback.
☐	☐	☐	9. Learners express themselves through writing and classroom discussion tied to learning.
☐	☐	☐	10. Assignments provide opportunities for individual choice.
☐	☐	☐	11. I provide timely, formative feedback to learners on the quality of their work.
☐	☐	☐	12. Supplementary learning options are available for struggling learners.
☐	☐	☐	13. Intervention takes place long before learners fail a class.
☐	☐	☐	14. Instruction is free of derogatory statements about individual cultures and backgrounds.
☐	☐	☐	15. I use examples in activities that reflect the cultural diversity of learners.
☐	☐	☐	16. I connect instruction to the daily lives of learners as well as to aspects of their community and life experiences.
☐	☐	☐	17. I accommodate learners' questions and interests in relation to lesson plans.

Active Learning Strategies — Tips and Techniques

While it sometimes may be efficient to have learners listen to a short lecture, view a video, or read a textbook, constantly doing these types of isolating, sedentary activities becomes a mind-numbing rather than mind-engaging practice. There are strategies that naturally contribute to a much higher level of learner engagement. For example, cooperative learning strategies in which learners are organized into structured discussion groups and play specific roles in the brainstorming process and in analyzing problems and seeking solutions are more engaging than listening to a long lecture. Moreover, varying instructional strategies adds interest and increases engagement. Even the most exciting activities, if done constantly, lose their appeal.

All teachers should incorporate active learning strategies in their classrooms. Active learning means that learners are more than passive receivers of knowledge; they become active participants in the thinking or discussion process. The importance of active learning strategies comes not only from observation of effective classrooms but also from current research on brain physiology. Modern technology has enabled biologists, medical researchers, and cognitive scientists to better understand how the human brain functions and how people learn.

By understanding how the brain develops, educators can create an enriched environment in which learners have opportunities to experiment and explore within the safe boundaries of the classroom. Experimentation and exploration will develop critical thinking and decision-making skills, preparing learners for the challenges that await them beyond school.

The brain is a vastly complex and adaptive system. Its 100 billion or so interconnecting neurons build patterns through synapses. The more frequently these patterns are used and enhanced through new experiences, the stronger they become. This is the process of learning.

Our brains seek meaning from the experiences around us. Learning that is relevant, meaningful, and connected to previous mental, emotional, and physical experiences strengthens memory. When the brain is challenged, learning is enhanced. For instance, instruction that uses emotion and physical energy engages many parts of the brain simultaneously and involves learners in the learning process. Brain research has confirmed that emotions are linked to learning by assisting in recall of memories that are stored in a person's central nervous system.

Enhance Active Learning

Following are some suggestions and pointers to enhance active learning in the classroom.

- **Engage all the senses**. The brain is stimulated through the senses. The more that teachers can create learning experiences that embody new sights, sounds, and manipulations, the more learning will occur. The brain records these many stimulations, but they are retained only as a result of rehearsal, practice, or connection to other knowledge and experiences. Each of the five senses — hearing, sight, touch, smell, and taste — plays a role in the learning process.

    ○ **Hearing.** Learners convert sounds such as the spoken word into meaningful information. Teacher lectures and discussions among learners and teachers provide sources of knowledge through listening.

    ○ **Sight.** Visual images contribute a great deal to the information that learners store as a part of their learning. For example, a digital slide presentation of key points or pictures reinforces what is to be learned from a short lecture and increases the likelihood that learners will remember what is being taught.

    ○ **Touch.** Certain skills and some types of work and recreation require the act of physically doing something to acquire knowledge. A musician or athlete acquires skills primarily through the act of playing the instrument or sport. The physical task of writing, as another example, reinforces many cognitive skills.

    ○ **Smell and taste.** The senses of smell and taste also lead to acquisition of knowledge. We all have vivid memories connected to certain smells (such as a campfire) and certain tastes or particular food items that remind us of past events.

- **Movement is key to learning**. We typically think that learning is purely a cognitive sedentary process, but physical movement is important to learning. Elementary teachers often involve learners in total physical instruction to incorporate movement. Learners of all ages benefit from physical movement to enhance brain activity and learning.

- **Storytelling is one of the best and oldest forms of teaching**. Our brains are wired to recall stories. Stories appeal to many learners and help them understand complex ideas, remember long lists, and grasp important themes. Elementary teachers frequently use stories, but this technique diminishes in secondary schools. With so many visual and auditory tools using computer technology, teachers should consider converting complex ideas into memorable stories. Use stories to emphasize important points, capture learner interest, make difficult concepts easier to grasp, and add an emotional connection to what otherwise would be less interesting material. Teachers can advance and enhance their storytelling skills by the dramatic use of voice, body gestures, and eye contact with learners.

- **Games stimulate learner engagement**. Often the necessary acquisition and assessment of core knowledge create less-than-stimulating instruction. Introducing games, competitions, and contests as part of learning new material in any subject significantly heightens learner interest, regardless of age. Today, it is easy to create games with resource tools available via the computer and the Internet.

- **Field trips significantly stimulate learner learning.** Field trips create some of the most memorable experiences in education. They provide direct observation of events and real-world situations. With budget limitations and conservative approaches to risk-taking, field trips have become infrequent experiences. However, technology offers many creative opportunities to have virtual field trips, allowing learners to observe, explore, and learn in an highly engaged manner.

- **Role-playing is an excellent strategy for increasing learner engagement.** It may not be possible to create an authentic real-world experience in the classroom, but role-playing can be nearly as effective. By assigning situations and specific roles, learners can acquire a depth of knowledge about a historical event or complex issue. Role-playing also gives learners an opportunity to engage in personal interaction.

- **Incorporate humor in instructional practices.** Researchers are taking more seriously the connection between humor and learning. A well-presented joke, cartoon, or parody naturally holds people's attention. Recent brain research confirms that when someone laughs, his/her brain activity increases. Teachers should not be afraid to incorporate humor into their instruction. A joke or cartoon not only takes the drudgery out of instruction; it also increases learner retention, relieves tension and stress, and helps build rapport with learners. With effective use of the Internet, teachers can locate and collect cartoons and videos that can add humor to instruction. Be cautious, however: Avoid humor that puts down learners, cultures, or any groups of individuals.

Making Learning Stick

In *Made to Stick: Why Some Ideas Survive and Others Die,* Chip Heath and Dan Heath describe the "stickiness factor" with six characteristics, all of which can be used to enhance active learning strategies.

- **Simplicity.** One of the most effective ways to create learning that sticks is to present information in a simple manner that builds on the knowledge learners already have. When teachers are deeply knowledgeable about the content of their subject matter, it is difficult to step outside of that knowledge to look at a lesson from a learner's perspective. Teachers who can build a lesson that starts with what learners already know and then simplify the underlying concepts are much more able to engage their learners.

- **Unexpectedness.** Learners remember messages, activities, and events that are unique and that contain an element of surprise. Teachers may create highly engaged lessons in which they dress like Abraham Lincoln to talk about the

Emancipation Proclamation or put on a Halloween costume to describe the characteristics of a living cell. These examples of humorous and colorful performances create memorable lessons. This is not to say that teachers need to dress in costumes or constantly entertain learners; but when they change a routine or teach a lesson in a new way, they create learning experiences that are more likely to stick.

- **Concreteness.** The more that teachers can offer metaphors, connections, and specific examples to illustrate a concept, the more likely learners will be to understand and remember what is being taught. For example, it is difficult for some learners to understand the three-dimensional structure of cells and how they form tissues or organs. Creating gelatin models of cells with bits of fruit as cell structures gives learners a concrete image that helps them visualize cell structure.

- **Credibility.** One strategy that advertisers use to emphasize the credibility of their products is employing well-known people in their marketing campaigns. Teachers can bring credibility to instruction by providing sources of endorsement beyond themselves and the textbook. Connecting learning to current events, local businesspeople, or other credible sources can help to affirm the realness of a particular lesson. For example, having a lab technician speak to a biology class about blood testing or a police detective discuss DNA evidence collection procedures makes a science lesson more interesting and credible.

- **Emotion.** Emotion, both on the part of the teacher and learner, influences learning. Most teachers recognize that their passion for their subject and their dedication to teaching have a significant impact upon learner engagement. If teachers do not appear excited and committed to instruction, it is no surprise that learners become disengaged. It is important for teachers to look for opportunities not only to express their enthusiasm but also to try to build an emotional connection for learners by showing how what learners are learning relates to their individual futures and their own situations.

- **Stories.** Creating lessons that include storytelling is an ideal way to enhance learner engagement. Storytelling is a powerful communication technique, but it is rarely practiced by teachers as part of classroom instruction. Stories illustrate, dramatize, and reinforce key concepts. When introducing stories, change the setting. While it is not necessary to put on a costume or prop such as a hat, doing so can add to the drama of the setting and help learners remember. Use a picture or other visual to add imagery to the story. Use local examples of places and people to help learners connect and put themselves in the story.

Active Learning Strategies

Brainstorming stimulates thinking; it allows learners to generate vast amounts of information and then to sort that information in a conversation with others.

Community service involves learning opportunities in which learners do unpaid work that adds value to the community and allows them to feel good about themselves.

Compare and contrast learning activities require analysis to identify similarities and differences.

Cooperative learning places learners in structured groups to solve problems by working cooperatively.

Creative arts are artistic products or performances that can be used to develop skills in classes other than art.

Games are exciting, structured activities that engage learners in individual or group competitions to demonstrate knowledge or complete an academic task.

Group discussion is any type of verbal dialogue among learners that explores ideas related to an instructional topic.

Inquiry engages learners in posing questions and making observations in an intriguing investigation that also encourages group dialogue.

Instructional technology— independent learning refers to the use of multimedia computer applications that enable the tailoring of programs directed toward learner questions or interests.

Internship is a formal placement in an employment situation for additional learning while the learner is still in school.

Presentations/exhibitions are oral demonstrations in which learners organize ideas and then express those ideas in their own words.

Problem-based learning introduces concepts by applying problem-solving skills to a real-world problem or investigation.

Self-processing allows learners to organize and internalize information by making connections to their own experiences.

Project design requires learners to integrate their skills and knowledge to create their own literary, technological, or artistic work as individuals or in a group.

Research means that learners locate and retrieve information from several sources, such as library references, textbooks, other individuals, and electronic databases.

Simulation/role-playing replicates the way that skills or knowledge are used outside school; it ranges from role-playing to computer-generated virtual reality.

Socratic seminars combine the elements of teacher questions, learner inquiry, and discussion around key topics.

Total physical response requires learners to engage in a physical activity as well as mental processes.

Work-based learning occurs when learners learn through on-the-job experiences, which range from job shadowing to full employment.

Multiple Intelligences

> The most important thing about curriculum differentiation is that it respects and responds to learner differences.
>
> — *Jeanne Purcell, education consultant*

> How many learners were rendered callous to ideas, and how many lost the impetus to learn because of the way in which learning was experienced by them?
>
> — *John Dewey*

Teachers should become familiar with the descriptions of the nine multiple intelligences, as defined by renowned education researcher Howard Gardner. (See *Intelligence Reframed: Multiple Intelligences for the 21st Century*.) It is not the teachers' task to analyze or diagnose the specific intelligences of each learner; teachers simply need to scatter the many ways of learning throughout academic learning experiences. Traditional one-size-fits-all teaching reaches only the 20% of learners who learn through Verbal/Linguistic and Logical/ Mathematical methods.

With most instruction concentrated on Verbal/Linguistic and Logical/Mathematical intelligences, learners with strong aptitudes in the other seven intelligences are likely to lose interest and even drop out of school if they do not have opportunities to apply and further develop their talents in the secondary years. These learners simply have different ways of knowing and learning than do the learners who learn primarily through Verbal/Linguistic and Logical/Mathematical intelligences. These learners are not failing — their schools are failing to reach and engage them. Following are lists of suggested activities that align with these nine intelligences. This list is adapted from *Engaging All by Creating High School Learning Communities*, by Jeanne Gibbs and Teri Ushijima.

Verbal/Linguistic

- Write story problems.
- Create TV advertisements.
- Compile a notebook of jokes.
- Debate current/historical issues.
- Play Trivial Pursuit™.
- Explain a situation/problem.
- Write poems.
- Present impromptu speaking/writing.
- Create crossword puzzles.
- Teach "concept mapping."
- Learn a foreign language.
- Write instructions.
- Read stories to others.
- Describe an object for someone to draw.
- Make up a story about a piece of music.
- Describe the steps to a dance.
- Write a role-play/drama.
- Keep a personal journal.

Logical/Mathematical

- Create a time line.
- Compare/contrast ideas.
- Predict the next events in a story.
- Define patterns in history.
- Follow a recipe/instructions.
- Rank the order of factors.
- Analyze causes and effects.
- Learn patterns.
- Analyze similarities/differences.
- Classify biological specimens.
- Create outlines of stories.
- Create computer programs.
- Use a story grid/creative writing.
- Create a paint-by-number picture.
- Read/design maps.
- Solve math problems.
- Teach calculator/computer use.
- Decipher codes.

Visual/Spatial

- Make visual diagrams/flow charts.
- Illustrate a story/historical event.
- Design/paint murals.
- Imagine the future/go back in time.
- Play Pictionary™.
- Teach "mind mapping" for note-taking.
- Write/decipher codes.
- Graph results of a survey.
- Create posters/flyers.
- Create collages on topics.
- Draw maps.
- Study the arts of a culture.
- Make clay maps/buildings/figures.
- Create visual diagrams/machines.
- Illustrate dance steps/physical games.

- Learn spatial games.
- Draw from different perspectives.
- Draw to music.
- Compose music from a matrix.

Interpersonal

- Role-play a historical/literary or class situation.
- Analyze a story.
- Tell stories.
- Read poetry using different moods.
- Teach arithmetic, math, computer skills.
- Review a book orally.
- Act out a different cultural perspective.
- Design and act out dramas/role-plays.
- Help a group come to a consensus or resolve a problem.
- Facilitate participation in a group.
- Play cooperative games.
- Help people deliver appreciation statements.
- Solve complex story problems.
- Discuss/debate controversial issues.
- Analyze group dynamics/relationships.
- Learn to sing and lead rounds.
- Plan and arrange social events.
- Find relationships among objects.

Existential

- Engage in reflection and self-study.
- Read books about the meaning of life.
- Attend some form of worship.
- Watch films on big "life questions."
- Record thoughts in a journal.
- Listen to inspirational music.
- Study literature, art, and philosophy.
- Discuss life/human issues in a group.
- Record dreams and mystical events.
- Paint while listening to music.
- Create a private "centering" space.

Naturalist

- Keep a journal of observations.
- Collect and categorize data.
- Make a taxonomy of plants or animals.
- Explain similarities among species.
- Study the means of survival.
- Examine cellular structures with a microscope.
- Illustrate cellular material.
- Take outdoor field trips.
- Visit an aquarium.
- Camp outside to identify stars.

Body/Kinesthetic

- Lead energizers and cooperative games.
- Practice physical exercises.
- Lead learners in stretching to music, deep breathing, tai chi, and yoga poses.
- Learn dances of different cultures and periods of history.
- Practice aerobic routines to fast music.
- Measure items or distances with thumbs, feet, or hands.
- Illustrate geometrical figures (parallel lines, triangles, rectangles, circles) with arms, legs and/or fingers.
- Coach peers and/or younger children.
- Conduct hands-on experiments.
- Act out scenes from stories or plays.
- Design role-plays.
- Invent a new household tool.
- Prepare food or snacks.
- Simulate various situations.
- Learn the alphabet through physical movement.
- Learn/teach sign language.
- Make up a cooperative playground game.

Musical/Rhythmic

- Create "raps" (key dates, math, poems).
- Teach songs from different cultures and eras.
- Play musical instruments.
- Make simple musical instruments.

- Learn through songs and jingles.
- Learn through drum beats/rhythm.
- Make up sounds and sound effects.
- Practice impromptu music.
- Create interpretive dance to music.
- Lead singing (songs from different cultures).
- Write to music.
- Reduce stress with music.
- Teach rhythm patterns from different cultures.
- Compose music for a dramatic production.
- Teach dance steps.
- Identify social issues through lyrics.
- Illustrate different moods through dance steps.
- Lead physical exercise to music.
- Clap a rhythm for the class to repeat.

Intrapersonal

- Keep a personal journal or feelings diary.
- Analyze historical personalities.
- Write about personal learning experiences.
- Evaluate personal and group strengths/weaknesses.
- Analyze thinking patterns.
- Understand group dynamics.
- Use, design, or lead guided imagery.
- Write an autobiography.
- Analyze literary characters and historical personalities.
- Define personal reflection questions.
- Imagine and write about the future.
- Dance to represent different stages in life.
- Practice relaxation techniques.
- Imagine self as character in history or story.
- Illustrate feelings/moods.
- Listen attentively.
- Draw self at different periods in life.
- Share how music affects feelings.
- Observe self (metacognition perspective).

Active Learning Self-Check

Always	Sometimes	Rarely	
☐	☐	☐	1. Learners collaborate in groups to accomplish meaningful tasks.
☐	☐	☐	2. Learners discuss/solve open-ended questions/ problems.
☐	☐	☐	3. I shift activities and strategies every 15–20 minutes to keep learners' attention.
☐	☐	☐	4. Learners are engaged in hands-on activities when appropriate.
☐	☐	☐	5. Learners are engaged in higher-order thinking activities.
☐	☐	☐	6. I model instructional strategies for active learning (for example, posing questions, experimenting, considering alternatives).
☐	☐	☐	7. I challenge learners to think deeply and critically.
☐	☐	☐	8. I draw on learners' interest when introducing a lesson.
☐	☐	☐	9. I facilitate learners' active construction of meaning (rather than simply telling).
☐	☐	☐	10. I use technology frequently and appropriately in instruction.
☐	☐	☐	11. I use a variety of resources and ways to promote understanding, such as audio or video sources, the Internet, and class demonstration.
☐	☐	☐	12. I use questioning, coaching, and feedback to stimulate learner reflection.
☐	☐	☐	13. Instruction is learner-centered, emphasizing learner choice of materials and activities, interaction, and construction of knowledge.

Focus on Reading — Tips and Techniques

> The more you read, the more things you will know.
> The more that you learn, the more places you'll go.
>
> — *Dr. Seuss*

It may seem unusual to talk about literacy, particularly reading, as a key ingredient in learner engagement. However, many successful schools emphasize the importance of focusing on literacy instruction for continuous learning in all subjects.

Having a literacy focus means that all teachers, regardless of their subject area, know the reading levels of the material that they are using, whether it is incorporated into textbooks, classroom directions, Internet-based resources, or other reading sources. Teachers also know the reading levels of their learners. Therefore, they are able to match reading materials in the classroom with individual learners and identify any significant gaps that might require a change in instructional strategy.

Teachers also need to incorporate vocabulary strategies as part of their instruction. Paying attention to specific terms related to a topic of discussion and using strategies to introduce and reinforce the vocabulary leads to comprehension and better learner engagement in every subject. Teachers need to use comprehension strategies, such as prereading and summarization, that provide an opportunity for learners to become more engaged in a required piece of reading for a particular instructional activity.

Reading is fundamental, and it cuts across all learning. If teachers expect high levels of learner engagement, they need to pay attention to reading levels and to establish instructional strategies with literacy as a primary focus in all they do.

Reading in the Content Areas

An increasing number of learners are ill equipped to read and comprehend the textbooks designed for proficient high school readers. Teachers recognize this fact well. What may not be so widely accepted, however, is the idea that content-area teachers can assist struggling readers. This does not mean that these teachers should become reading teachers, but it does mean that they can structure lessons to assist struggling readers.

In most school districts, formal reading instruction on a regular, systematic basis ends in 6th grade, when the focus on "learning to read" shifts to literary appreciation and "reading to learn." Content material becomes a focus of everyday reading activity in grades 7–12, yet no consistent effort is made to teach learners how to improve their reading and to comprehend content. Even in elementary school, all teachers should connect reading instruction with instruction in science, social studies, and other areas of the curriculum.

While content-area teachers often are the first to recognize the problem of inadequate reading skills, most feel unprepared to address the issue because they lack training in teaching reading. Moreover, with the increasing pressures of proficiency testing, they are concerned that reading instruction will take time away from the primary subject that they are responsible for teaching.

In middle schools and high schools, textbooks and other instructional materials are content driven, with no uniform degree of reading difficulty. Teachers typically select the text that covers the content, not the text that is most appropriate for the reading levels, interests, or ongoing proficiency development levels of most learners. Each subject is likely to have its own concepts, specialized vocabulary (sometimes hundreds of new words), forms, formats, document types, and visual aids, all presented through a variety of text sources and writing styles. When homework is assigned, learners are expected to read the textbook on their own, organize and synthesize information, and present it in a written format.

Why are teachers and parents surprised when learners become frustrated and unmotivated? Consider the challenges that learners face:

- **Concept density.** More ideas and skills are squeezed into an already overloaded curriculum.

- **Specialized forms and formats.** Informational presentation and reporting devices either are general conventions of informational documentation or are specific to a subject.

- **Specialized vocabulary.** Terms typically have multiple meanings or are unique to a particular text.

- **Graphs/charts/maps**. More functional graphic organizers and presentation tools are used to convey increasingly complex information, requiring learners' interpretation.

- **Purpose for reading**. Learners need to shift purposes as they deal with facts, summaries, glossaries, formulas, and highlighted text.

- **Readability.** The readability levels of many texts are higher than learner reading skill levels.

- **Length.** Texts are long and comprehensive.

- **Nonprint sources.** Searching and selecting online references, formats, and other sources requires special skills.

- **Instructional materials**. Teachers choose materials without knowing the reading difficulty levels or the ability levels of their learners.

How can teachers help learners face the challenges of reading to learn? What are the habits and skills of effective readers in middle schools and high schools? The answer lies in teaching reading strategies to engage learners in content, maintain their focus, and improve their understanding and application of what they have read. When learners have appropriate skills to complete the task before them, strategic reading takes place, in which they are able to:

- understand and use textbook aids
- select strategies that ensure effective processing of information
- monitor their learning
- reflect on their learning

Learners who are strategic readers are able to demonstrate a repertoire of strategies automatically, independently, and in a variety of ways. Effective readers use these cognitive processes and strategies competently and unconsciously to achieve academically. These strategies affect the processing of text, enhancing the ability of the reader to retrieve, remember, and use the material. Examples of strategies include outlining, note-taking, highlighting, underlining, summarizing, and questioning.

Effective readers at the secondary school level:

- devote time to previewing material before reading
- seek to control the time, place, and location best suited for their learning

- develop multiple learning strategies that apply to a variety of reading assignments
- understand their ability to concentrate and adjust their reading times into smaller units
- employ techniques to recite, retell, or summarize orally what they are reading
- engage in a process of "self-talk" to identify important statements and text structure that aid comprehension
- engage in reflective questioning to ensure active processing of the material

Teachers need to assist learners in learning how to use strategies intuitively so that learners can move from frustrated novices to competent readers. Each task needs to be tackled with the knowledge of:

- the type of reading material being encountered
- the purpose of the reading task
- the demands of the specific type of content
- available strategies for the reader to use

Reading a history textbook requires readers to employ different strategies from what they would use when reading the owner's manual for a DVD player. The history book requires readers to understand cause and effect, for example, rather than follow the step-by-step procedure found in an owner's manual. Equally different are the tasks involved in reading mathematics textbooks, science textbooks, test forms, applications, school newspapers, online reference sources, and learner handbooks, to name a few.

Learners who do not automatically employ reading strategies struggle with written material throughout their lives. It is the job of educators to teach all learners how to acquire and apply a wide variety of reading strategies across a wide range of forms, genres, and types of content to ensure that they become independent, competent readers. Following are some suggested strategies.

- **Offer reading options.** Try to balance required reading with learners' desire to have some control over what they read. It is easy to assign uniform required reading; it is more effective for engagement to give learners some choice.
- **Model continuous reading.** Teachers need to make it evident to learners that they themselves read constantly. Have books around, refer to recent reading, and read with learners. Also be open to other forms of reading, including digital reading, that may provide related information to the topic at hand.
- **Use graphic organizers.** Make it easy for learners to visually record and interpret information such as characters and plots in literature, cause and effect in science, and timelines in history.

The Before, During, and After Approach to Reading

Following a framework of "before," "during," and "after" reading strategies helps teachers to give learners a clear idea about what they need to accomplish to become successful, lifelong readers. The Before, During and After Approach to Reading contains the following strategic elements:

Before Reading

Activating background knowledge. Learners are taught to elicit prior knowledge of the reading topic. They build a background relating to what they already know. Questions that learners can use to inventory their prior knowledge might include:

- What do I already know about mammals?
- What have I read, heard, or watched about mammals?
- What other words do I think of when I see the word *mammals*?

Investigating text structure. Learners are taught to analyze the text before them — its print features, layout, and illustrations. They are taught to consider the language and the literary features of the text. They learn to discriminate between narrative and expository text.

- Does the author use headings and subheadings?
- Does the author use illustrations, graphs, tables, or maps?
- Are important words highlighted or italicized?

Setting a purpose for reading. Learners are taught to ask themselves why they are reading the material.

- What is my goal?
- What questions do I need to answer after reading?
- What will I do with the information from the reading?
- What do I want to learn from reading this?

After learners determine their own purpose for reading, they then can select their own reading style to best suit the purpose. They decide whether to skim to get an overview, scan to locate specific information, or read and reread to recall details. They also are taught to determine the author's purpose in writing the selection.

Predicting the text content. Learners are taught to form ideas about what is going to happen in the text. They learn how to combine and use the information that they are reading to make meaningful guesses about the material.

- What do I already know about the topic?
- How can I combine my knowledge with clues in the text?
- How will making predictions help me understand this material better?

Reviewing and clarifying vocabulary. Learners are taught to use word-solving strategies to pronounce a word correctly and understand its meaning.

- How do other words in the sentence give me clues about pronouncing this word?
- How do other words in the sentence give me clues about understanding the meaning of this word?
- How do the sentences before and after help me solve the word in this sentence?

During Reading

During the reading process, learners establish a purpose for each part of the text. They are taught to ask themselves why they are reading a particular text or passage — whether it is to retell, answer questions, gather information, make comparisons, or to get the main idea.

- What is my purpose for reading this chapter?
- Do I need to define and understand the meaning of terms?
- Do I need to identify the main idea?
- Do I need to participate in a discussion?
- Do I need to summarize important ideas?
- Do I need to confirm predictions?

Self-monitoring. Learners are taught to check themselves while they are involved in the reading process. They ask themselves if what they are reading makes sense. They learn how to self-correct to monitor their accuracy.

- How does what I am reading fit with what I am understanding?
- What information do I need to understand better?
- Did what I just read make sense?
- Do I need to go back and reread to understand?

Visualizing. Learners are taught to create mental images that can help them to construct details, leading to comprehension.

- Can I see in my head what the author is trying to explain or describe?

Summarizing. Learners are taught to stop and think during their reading to determine who or what they read about and where the action is taking place.

- What were the most important ideas on the page that I just read?
- How were the ideas related to each other?

Confirming or rejecting predictions. Learners are taught to revise predictions made before reading, using the information gathered during their reading. They learn to locate evidence to assist them in confirming or rejecting the predictions they made.

Identifying and clarifying key ideas. Learners are taught to reflect on information, ideas, and words as they read. They learn how to think about what they are reading, how to reread for clarity, and how to distinguish between important and less important information in the text.

- What was important in what I just read?
- What did I already know, and what information was new?
- How can I combine sections to get a deeper understanding?

Questioning. Learners are taught to use the text to answer different kinds of questions that the teacher poses. They learn to distinguish among literal, inferential, and critical types of questions.

- Is this a question for which I can find the answer "right there" in the text?
- Is this a question that I need to answer by combining information that I already have with clues from the text?
- Is this a question that requires my opinion and reasons for that opinion?

After Reading

Assessing whether the purpose was met. Learners are taught to recall the before-reading process, to decide whether they met the purpose, and to determine what to do if they did not accomplish the goal.

- Did I accomplish my purpose for reading this text?
- Did the author accomplish his/her purpose for writing it?

Paraphrasing. Learners are taught to interpret and restate the author's ideas, using information from the reading and their own knowledge. They learn how to rewrite the author's ideas in their own words.

- What ideas do I want to remember and/or share?
- How can I put each idea into my own words without leaving out important details?

Identifying main ideas and details. Learners are first taught to identify facts or ideas that are relevant to understanding and then to use that information to select the primary focus of the text.

- What is the most important idea in the text?
- Which details support that idea?

Making comparisons. Learners are taught to compare and contrast information within a text and between texts. They learn how to look for similarities and differences.

- What other information is this like?
- How is this information different from other ideas in this book?
- How is this information similar to other sources?
- How is this information different from other sources?

Connections. Learners are taught to draw on their own experiences to help clarify the text. They learn how to connect to experiences or relationships to further construct meaning.

- How can I combine this new information with what I already know?
- Where, when, why, and how did I see or use this information before?
- How can what I know help me understand these new ideas?

Drawing conclusions. Learners are taught to add textual and/or visual clues to the information they already have acquired to reach a conclusion.

- What has the text implied?
- How can I use the clues in the text and the ideas in my head to understand the overall meaning?

Summarizing. Learners are taught to create brief statements about reading passages and entire selections. They learn how to extract and organize the important information gained from their reading.

- What information do I need to remember?
- How can I sort the ideas to make good sense?
- Which ideas can I connect?

Analyzing. Learners are taught to make judgments about what they read and to support their ideas with explicit information from the text.

- How did all the information fit together?
- What reaction do I have to the author's stance?
- Why do I feel the same or differently about the topic?

The Before, During and After Approach to Reading is an important part of a lesson or unit design. Teachers spend their preparation time searching for reading selections that match learners' reading levels and that relate to the topic of the lesson objective. Teachers assess throughout the activity to correct misconceptions and address questions about the topic. (For more information, see these International Center resources: *Effective Instructional Strategies for Content Area Reading in Grades 7–12* and *Effective Instructional Strategies for Content Area Writing in Grades 7–12*.)

Matching Text to Learner Reading Levels

Reading is to the mind what exercise is to the body.

— *Richard Steele, Irish writer and politician*

If learners are not engaged in reading, it may be because the reading level is too difficult or too easy. Even if text is appropriately matched to learner reading levels, learners may be having trouble using a comprehension skill (such as cause and effect, main idea, key terms and definitions, using context clues to define difficult terms, and so on). Review specific skills, such as those previously described, for learners as needed. Continue to work on any subskills that seem to be giving learners difficulty until reading comprehension is no longer a problem.

Assume that learner reading levels will change or will vary by type of format or content being read or according to learner interest or prior knowledge of the subject. Continue to monitor learner results on exams and class presentations to determine whether learners are ready to move to a higher reading level. Learners must show fluency (reading automatically without having to decode or use brain power to figure out new words) before they are ready for the challenge of the next level.

Monitor learner performance at least twice a month and make adjustments to the level of learner reading selections as needed. As teachers frequently and appropriately monitor and adjust reading selections based upon learner performance, they will see reading comprehension and class performance continue to rise.

The Lexile® Framework for Reading

The Lexile® Framework for Reading, developed by MetaMetrics®, Inc., in conjunction with several leading U.S. universities, is an excellent tool for teachers to:

- select text in articles or textbooks that is matched to individual reading levels
- cluster or group individuals with similar reading levels

The Framework uses a computer program called the Lexile Analyzer® to examine and analyze the readability of a whole text, not just samples from it. The Analyzer measures such characteristics as sentence length (a highly reliable proxy for syntactic complexity) and semantic difficulty (recognized vocabulary measured against high frequency word lists); it then reports a Lexile® measure for the text. Documents that have been analyzed receive a score on a scale from 200L to 2000L. (Very simple documents that would score below 200L are deemed unsuitable for this analysis because they do not contain a sufficient amount of text.) Lexile measures for some well-known works of literature include *Frog and Toad Are Friends* — 400L; *War and Peace* — 1200L; and *The Scarlet Letter* — 1400L. The middle 50% of learners in 4th grade typically have Lexile measures between 445L and 810L; in 8th grade, between 805L and 1100L; and in 11th and 12th grade, between 940L and 1210L.

Unlike grade-equivalent measures of readability, the Lexile scale is based on uniform increments of 100L, which is constant in terms of appropriate increases in semantic and syntactic complexity. A one-grade difference expressed in grade equivalents, however, is not. For example, the difference in reading difficulty between 3.2 and 4.2 may be much greater than the one-grade difference between 9.2 and 10.2. Moreover, Lexile measures avoid the problem of labeling reading expectations for a particular grade level. Referencing Lexile measures also reinforces the notion that reading abilities differ broadly within any grade.

Publishers of educational tests use Lexile measures for learner readability measures and testing reports. By equating Lexile measures with test scores, Lexile equivalent measures have been determined for millions of learners, and they continue to be reported on widely administered achievement tests used across the nation. As a result, MetaMetrics has established Lexile measures for learners at each grade level. For example, the measure for the middle 50% of learners in grades 11–12 is between 940L and 1210L. Working with a wide variety of educational publishers, MetaMetrics also has analyzed the readability levels of textbooks and numerous other instructional materials. There clearly is a gap between learners' reading levels and the readability level of the texts that they must read in school. Of the learners in grades 11–12, 25% read below 940L, yet typical instructional materials range between 1100L and 1300L.

Many states and several national standardized test providers already have enlisted the Lexile Framework to provide individual learner reading levels as part of the reporting process to districts and teachers on the standardized testing results report. This means that when each learner gets his/her results on achievement tests, a Lexile reading level is reported. Lexile levels also can be determined by using the Scholastic Reading Inventory or the Northwest Evaluation Association MAPS assessment.

This Lexile research underscores what teachers already recognize: Learners in the same classroom have different levels of reading proficiency, yet all of them typically read the same materials. The result is a mismatch for many learners, who cannot learn from textbooks that they cannot read. For them, this mismatch means lower comprehension, lower test scores, and less progress in attaining proficiency — not just in reading, but across the curriculum. Once teachers know the learners' Lexile measure, they can help the learners choose text written in their Lexile range (50L below to 150L above the established reading level). Using the Lexile measures not only helps learners whose reading skills are lacking, but it also improves the skills of learners who are competent and exceptional readers. A comprehensive reading program should include both independent reading and instructional reading practices.

Reading Self-Check

Always	Sometimes	Rarely	
☐	☐	☐	1. Literacy is an important priority in my teaching.
☐	☐	☐	2. I have convenient access to data about my learners' reading levels.
☐	☐	☐	3. I know the reading levels reflected in the textbooks and other instructional materials that I use.
☐	☐	☐	4. I make selections of instructional materials to challenge learners appropriately.
☐	☐	☐	5. I make accommodations or provide support for learners below target reading levels.
☐	☐	☐	6. Learners are introduced to charts and images as part of literacy-focused instruction.
☐	☐	☐	7. I use learner dialogue and collaboration to improve comprehension.
☐	☐	☐	8. I use graphic organizers appropriate to my content area to extend learner thinking and understanding about information from any source.
☐	☐	☐	9. I use video clips and other resources to improve my learners' background knowledge before assigning a reading task.
☐	☐	☐	10. I have introduced at least two note-taking methods to help my learners organize and synthesize information.
☐	☐	☐	11. I teach learners literacy strategies and gradually empower them to select strategies that help them understand and communicate.
☐	☐	☐	12. I expect learners to write every day.
☐	☐	☐	13. I know the difficult and new vocabulary in my instruction and introduce this to learners in advance of a reading assignment.
☐	☐	☐	14. I use effective vocabulary strategies such as having learners write definitions in their own terms, apply them in writing assignments, and identify synonyms.
☐	☐	☐	15. I use prereading and postreading strategies to improve reading comprehension.

Reading Self-Check (Continued)

Always	Sometimes	Rarely	
☐	☐	☐	16. I know the reading level requirements for postsecondary opportunities, including college, employment, and personal use.
☐	☐	☐	17. I personalize instruction to accommodate different levels of reading in the classroom.
☐	☐	☐	18. I challenge learners to increase reading fluency and comprehension.
☐	☐	☐	19. I know the reading level of state assessments at my grade level and in my subject area.

 **Chapter 7**

Technology Solutions

Using Technology to Engage Learners

For teachers seeking to increase learner engagement, technology is an important consideration. Well-known author and digital game designer Mark Prensky refers to today's kindergarten through college learners as "digital natives." These learners are the first generation to grow up with the culture of computers, videogames, iPods, PDAs, and all the other gadgets of the digital age. On the other hand, many adults are more like "technology immigrants," having had to learn the language of new technologies in order to communicate via blogs, wikis, texting, Facebook, or video.

Today's learners, immersed from the start in this technology-rich environment, are fluent in technology's many tools and facets; they cannot imagine a world without pervasive, rapid technology. As such, learners are naturally more comfortable than adults are in using and adapting to new information technology tools. They are critical of instruction that avoids using technology. They are also extremely uncomfortable when we demand that they unplug and put away their phones, music players, and games.

Technology is inherently more engaging than other instructional strategies for the following reasons:

- Learners are comfortable with technology; they use it all the time.
- Technology is multisensory; it includes visuals, sounds, colors, motion, and the use of touch and/or manipulation. This multisensory format stimulates more of the brain and is naturally more engaging to learners.
- Technology often gives learners choices and encourages them to use their creativity — another key factor in learner engagement.

The degree to which technology is beneficial in engaging learners depends on the way it is applied in the classroom and beyond. When used effectively, it presents great possibilities for expanding engagement. Technology offers learners a chance to delve deeply into a topic. Greater accessibility to information gives learners the opportunity to gather information easily and to analyze and synthesize information in new ways. Learners can manipulate information to identify the portions that are relevant to their needs. They can use information from one subject area in another, integrating the information to enhance their understanding. Doing so gives them greater control over their learning.

Computers, mobile devices, and the Internet provide teachers with tools to create their own teaching materials, to go beyond what is in the textbook and use alternate resources, and to organize information in new ways. Technology can be helpful to teachers because it accommodates various learning styles and can enhance instructional strategies in many ways.

Even families that have limited resources still may give learners access to technology. Ask your learners about their technology use. Use their responses to make decisions about how to use technology to engage learners, taking advantage of their technological skills and interests.

Here are some questions to ask:

- Why do you use the Internet (top three reasons)?
- What technology devices do you own (computer, mobile device, game console)?
- How do you access the Internet (home computer, mobile device)?
- How often are you online (frequency and length of time)?

Linking Technology to the Rigor/Relevance Framework

Technology should be integrated in a way that increases the rigor and relevance of instruction. Moreover, examining how learners are using technology makes it possible to identify the level of rigor and relevance of learning. The different ways in which technology is used can be linked to the quadrants of the Rigor/Relevance Framework. The following figure shows the different roles that learners take in each of the quadrants.

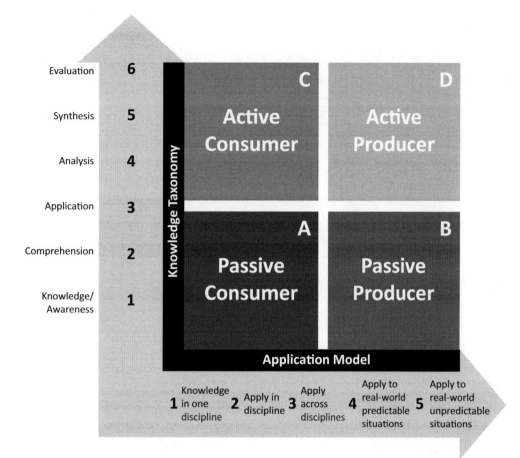

When working in Quadrant A (low rigor/low relevance), the learner is a passive consumer of the technology. When working in Quadrant B, the learner becomes a passive producer, using the technology to complete some task or procedure. The learner is producing something, yet with limited innovation or creativity.

In Quadrant C, the learner is an active consumer of technology. The learner is active, but the technology is not essential to the work. The learner may choose to use the technology to complete the work more efficiently, such as researching a topic and writing a report. In Quadrant D (high rigor/high relevance), the learner is active, but this time as more of a producer than a consumer of technology. Here, the learner creates a product through the use of technology.

Technology Applications for Rigorous and Relevant Learning

6

5

4

Quadrant C Assimilation

- Use the Internet to research problems or research questions.
- Use computer or mobile device for reference of decisions and expert systems.
- Create and display graphic organizers of solutions to complex problems.
- Engage in complex simulations to apply decision-making skills.
- Use a computer or mobile device to keep track of brainstorming.
- Engage in online discussions of group projects and problems.

Quadrant D Adaptation

- Create project designs and model solutions on computer or mobile device.
- Use calculators and computers for calculating design data.
- Use robots to conduct design tests.
- Use the Internet to collect information on design needs.
- Engage in discussion of real-world issues with students of other nations through the Internet.
- Produce visuals as part of student presentations of major projects.
- Design Web pages for actual customers.

3

2

1

Quadrant A Acquisition

- Use an online game to test knowledge of vocabulary.
- Use drill and practice applications to reinforce fundamental skills.
- Tutor students to catch up on content that they have not yet mastered.
- View demonstrations through animation, remote video, or apps.
- Use computer or mobile device visuals to illustrate lectures.
- Use word processing or note taking apps for taking notes.
- Make reference notes available for students on the Internet.
- Use a digital whiteboard to record classroom notes and discussion.
- Create graphic organizers and visual displays of information.
- Distribute note-taking templates and assignments to students via networks.

Quadrant B Application

- Use word processing or publishing applications to produce newsletters, brochures, and so forth.
- Design Web pages.
- Use e-mail to contact and interview experts.
- Edit video and audio clips.
- Use heart monitors to record exercise impacts.
- Use electronic diagnostic equipment with automobiles.
- Locate technical specifications in online databases.
- Create spreadsheets to record and analyze data.
- Use technology to compose and play music.
- Use word processing to edit the writing of others.

1   2   3   4   5

Expanding Possibilities

When used effectively, technology offers exciting possibilities for expanding learning beyond what schools have previously taught. Technology accommodates various learning styles. It puts vast amounts of knowledge at learners' fingertips. Databases on every subject imaginable are made available for study in all curriculum areas. Learners can use the Internet and reference software for researching topics and then can create presentations using multimedia software. Encyclopedias and complete collections of literary works on the Internet expand the walls of classrooms to encompass the world.

Learners can also manipulate and reorder what they learn, giving them greater control over their learning. Information technology links curriculum with real-world experiences, both inside and outside the school. Using the Internet, learners can work together in cooperative learning situations to help solve real problems, tying their education to real-life situations and giving them invaluable learning experiences.

Examples of Engaging Learners Through Technology

Learner Presentations

- Give learners the option of creating audio and/or video podcasts to deliver reports and summaries of research. Learners are comfortable using multimedia forms of communication.

- Have learners create digital postcards for a country they are studying (for example, in foreign language or geography classes).

- Have learners create narrations and videos about what they learned in class. Post these on a website to share with parents and the entire school.

- Use digital forms of storytelling. Have learners use pictures, text slides, animations, music, and sound effects to add to a story that they compose.

- Create project designs and model solutions on the computer.

- Have learners design Web pages for a community or school group project.

- Have learners use slides, animation, and video to supplement and enhance their presentations and reports.

Learner Inquiry

- Use adaptive technologies for special education learners.

- Use simulation software applications, such as *SimCity Societies* or *RockSim* (rocket simulation software), in which learners can make virtual decisions and follow through on the results of those decisions.

- Use videos to establish background in advance of reading assignments.

Learner Research

- Challenge learners to find accurate and inaccurate sources of information in Internet searches.

- When assigning online searches, make sure that learners use the online databases usually subscribed by the school rather than the often questionable quality of some Internet sources.

- Use calculators and spreadsheets to analyze and display research data.

- Use probes in science to collect real-world data.
- In physical education, use electronic devices to record heart rate, distance running, and calories burned to evaluate fitness routines.
- Use robots and simulators to conduct design tests.
- Use GIS software to have learners map various community resources.
- Have learners conduct online surveys of other learners and community members as part of a research project, and use spreadsheets to analyze and chart the data.

Class Discussions

- Allow learners to use portable remote response devices to reply to questions, and keep each learner responding and engaged.
- Engage learners in discussions of real-world issues with learners of other nations via the Internet.
- Establish peer-to-peer communication with e-mail groups, blogs, or wikis for discussion among learners in a class.
- Create blogs for groups of learners to discuss class projects and discussion questions.

Homework

- Put review tests and practice questions online. Learners enjoy seeing immediate feedback as they finish tests, and they like having copies of quizzes to study later on.
- Use digital whiteboards to display and record learner work in class. Make digital copies of work available for learners.
- Use commercially available podcasts from public television, news services, and other not-for-profit groups to supplement learner reading and provide more current information.
- Use social networking websites to set up class discussion groups for frequent communication among class members.
- Use digital recorders and players for learners to practice basic letter sounds or pronunciation of vocabulary words.
- Create a wiki of references that learners will need for various projects. Encourage learners to build on the information and to share new ideas and resources.

Learner Assessment

- Use technology-based games to review and practice recall of core knowledge.

- Have learners produce an electronic portfolio of their best work and showcase this work to parents as part of parent/teacher conferences.

- Use an iPod with voice recorder to record learner reading fluency. The learner reads a passage into the recorder. The captured voice memo files, when synced with iTunes, are transferred to the Voice Memos playlist in iTunes to create a digital record, or ePortfolio, of progress.

Teacher Presentations

- Create graphics of biological or Earth cycles or chemical reactions to reinforce understanding.

- Create animations and charts in mathematics to show relationships, patterns, and results of math equations.

- In physical education, use digital pictures and videos to demonstrate posture and review proper athletic techniques.

- Use technology-based timers and audio clips to control the beginning and end of activities, such as quizzes, warm-ups, and discussions.

 **Chapter 8**

Common Problems — Creative Solutions

Following are some strategies that address common teacher issues in the quest to raise learner engagement.

1. **How do I get learners focused to begin a lesson?**

   - Use literature to introduce scientific concepts or historical events.

   - Ask reflective questions pertaining to the topic, such as "What are similarities or differences between _____ and _____?" or "If _____ were changed, what do you think might have happened?"

   - Bring in an "artifact" that will intrigue learners — something unexpected that will stimulate questions.

   - Provide some type of "warm up" or "hook," such as a bell-ringer activity, intriguing observation, or inquiry problem, before beginning a lesson.

   - Present a real-world situation/problem and then get learners involved in solving it.

   - Give each learner an envelope with a task for an activity. Allow no talking until they have read the task; then give oral instructions for the activity.

   - Send learners an e-mail with questions to engage them.

   - Relate a lesson to learners' prior knowledge and experiences.

   - Capture interest with a good story.

   - Use a simple music, noise, or rhythm cue to focus the class.

2. **How can I create engaging lessons with limited teaching resources?**

   - Use games to review content.

   - Invite other teachers or parents to share relevant experiences.

- Have learners bring to class items that interest them, such as family photographs related to a history lesson or pets for a science lesson.
- Use the minutes from school board or government meetings for examples of problems to solve.
- Ask businesses for donations, such as scrap paper or computers.
- Have learners build a wiki or an online reference source for future classes to use.

3. **How do I deal with persistent learner absences?**

- Follow through in reporting excessive absenteeism to the administration.
- Use incentives, such as monthly attendance awards.
- Make learners feel important and wanted. When they return after an absence, tell them that you and the class have missed them.
- Contact parents to get them involved.
- Keep track of due dates for homework and require learners to make up work when they are absent.
- Institute intensive interventions for absentees, such as parent conferences and teacher group conferences with a counselor, even in early grades.
- Set reasonable attendance rules and consequences, such as allowing learners a minimal number of excused absences.
- Call the learner's home every time that he/she misses a class.
- Build good relationships with parents.
- Solicit businesses for rewards, such as discount coupons, for good attendance.

4. **How do I get learners to complete assignments?**

- Reward learners at the end of the week for completing all assignments.
- Highlight assignments in each learner's assignment book as a reminder of work not completed. Review the assignment books daily.
- Give fewer but more relevant assignments.
- Have an assignment board on the wall and use a marker to show assignments completed by each learner or by the class as a whole.
- Have clear consequences for failure to complete homework, and stick to them.
- Have incentives for completing homework, such as a "no homework" pass for completing homework regularly.
- Put a star on a chart for each completed assignment. When the chart is full, give a small prize or reward.
- Have learners work in teams to complete practice assignments.
- Have learners show you work completed.

- Reduce lunch period time for learners whose work is not completed.
- Have an exit requirement for learners to complete work before leaving class.
- Check homework as soon as learners enter class.

5. **How do I handle learners who are consistently disruptive and demand most of my intention?**

- Keep changing activities, and keep them interesting.
- Find out what interests the learners, and relate work/lessons to those interests.
- Use digital whiteboard technology for instruction.
- Allow learners more choices about how they carry out assignments.
- Give each learner a specific role when working in a group.
- Move learners to different areas several times during the course of a class.
- Reduce downtime.
- Keep learners involved through interesting lessons at their level.
- Break a project into small tasks that must be checked before moving on. Often, disruptive learners fail to see how they can accomplish a large, difficult project.
- Observe teachers who have gained control.
- Take lessons in classroom management; listen to suggestions from other teachers.
- Develop a social contract with each learner.
- Practice classroom procedures, such as forming small groups or reconvening as entire class.
- Establish consistent expectations and consequences at the beginning of the school year for the entire school.

6. **How do I engage learners with different learning styles or attention problems?**

- Learners with attention problems often need more physicality. Incorporate a variety of hands-on activities to encourage learners to use as many senses as possible.
- Vary the activities during a lesson.
- Include peer-grouping and partner activities.
- Promote technological activities.
- Incorporate small-group instruction.
- Incorporate project-based activities that have a hands-on component. These types of activities appeal to many learners who struggle to concentrate on bookwork.

7. **How do I handle learners whose persistent home/outside distractions are obstacles to engagement?**

    - Support learners privately in dealing with their issues. Building trust is an essential component of engaging learners in the classroom. One way to build trust is to take an interest in their personal lives.

    - Help a learner as much as you can; then refer the learner to counseling if needed.

    - Provide a pleasant and caring classroom atmosphere. Encourage learners to try to forget about outside problems for a while.

    - Work on parent communication throughout the year.

    - Be receptive to learners' needs. Give learners positive reinforcement of what they can be.

    - Provide "worry bags" — brown lunch bags assigned to each learner. Learners write notes about their problems and put the notes into their bag. At the end of the day, they can look at the bag and throw it away or talk about it.

    - Conduct periodic home visits.

    - Require learners to do journal writing.

    - Do daily checks on learner progress. Make sure that you praise learners and reassure them that they can do the work.

8. **How do I generate engagement with a crowded classroom and a large class size?**

    - Consider using hallways, the cafeteria, and school grounds.

    - Cluster desks and have learners do group work.

    - Trade classrooms temporarily with another teacher to provide more space for some critical activities.

    - Rearrange the room to make more space.

    - Use individual problem solving, giving learners problems to analyze and solve on their own.

    - Arrange learners in a circle for cooperative learning.

    - Use two- and four-person cooperative groups.

    - Think of mentally challenging ideas for group discussion.

9. **How do I create an engaging classroom when there is a lack of motivation and commitment to engagement in the school culture (varying discipline, rules, and procedures throughout the school)?**

    - Establish clear expectations and follow up.

    - Solicit support from the administration.

    - Create a learner handbook and teach it.

© International Center for Leadership in Education

- Make sure that rules are posted in as many places as possible and that the learner handbook is in a visible space for learners to review.
- Ask the district to address attendance concerns, and follow through.
- Create a learner council and get its members involved in aspects of social behavior and academic improvement.

10. **How do I solve the problem of learners' rushing to finish their work as quickly as possible without regard to quality?**

- Chunk assignments into smaller parts. Check partial assignments and provide feedback. Do not let learners move on until there is an acceptable level of quality.
- Conduct peer evaluations.
- Display learner work.
- Use stickers for recognition of high-quality work.
- Post completed high-quality assignments.
- Create relevant hands-on assignments.
- Use learners as assistants to review work and coach other learners.
- Create more challenging work; learners often are bored because they are underchallenged.
- Use various methods of testing, such as oral interviews or reflection journals.

11. **How do I solve cooperative group work issues in which one learner is working and the others are off-task?**

- Formulate balanced groups and give each learner an assignment suited to his/her strengths.
- Rotate groups frequently after the completion of assignments.
- Require learners to follow a rubric.
- Have the group grade each member for participation.
- Talk to each learner in a group on a regular basis to see how he or she is contributing.
- Assign a specific role (for example, recorder, speaker, researcher, or timekeeper) to each learner. Rotate duties.
- Stand closer to learners who appear not to be working.